THE FAVOUR OF GOD

T<small>HE</small> F<small>AVOUR OF</small> G<small>OD</small>

BY Pastor David Amoah

First published in 2015 by In The Way Publishing© Ltd, London ©Text 2015 David Amoah
Second edition with amendments published by Life and Success Publishing 2015.
The rights of David Amoah to be identified as author of this work have been asserted by him in accordance with the Copyright, Designs and Patents Acts 1988.

All rights reserved. No part of this publication may be reproduced, stored in a retrieval system or transmitted, in any form or by any means, electronic, mechanical or otherwise, without the prior written permission of the publisher.

ISBN: 978-1-907402-74-6

This book is sold subject to the condition that it may not be resold or otherwise issued except in its original binding.
The CIP catalogue record for this book is available from the British Library. British Library Cataloguing-in-Publishing Data.
All quotations are from the Holy Bible New International version and the New King James version unless otherwise stated.

Design: MIA Design
Editor: Mandi Gomez

DEDICATION

It is with delight that I dedicate this wonderful book to Mrs Agnes Saarah Mensah and Sister Evelyn Nyanteng Donkoh, both of Calvary Charismatic Baptist Church, London, UK. I offer my appreciation to God for His divine connection that brought these wonderful women into my life. God bless you my dear sisters.

Contents

Introduction 1

Jesus Christ: Our Ultimate Favour 7

The Benefits of Favour 22

Stories about the Benefits and
the Dangers of Favour 31

The Favour of
God Brings Prosperity 57

The Favour of
God Brings Revelation 62

The Favour of God Will Take You
to the Palace 67

The Assurance of Favour 115

Favour Brings Confidence 130

Favour can be Both Acquired and
Earned 136

The Dangers or the Risks of Favour 156

Those Who Risk Their Life and
Work to Favour Others 198

Conclusion 202

INTRODUCTION

Favour is something we all need in our daily lives. Everyone needs the favour of God, for if you are favoured by God you will receive the favour of men too. As a minister, I too need the favour of God; even politicians and people in high places, who need people to vote for them to acquire and maintain their position in life, need the favour of God, mostly because favour brings elevation.

The favour of God can turn any impossible situation into a possible one. The favour of God brings healing and the provision of God. The favour of God brings about change from the worst to the best. When you are favoured, it does not matter whether you are the eldest or the youngest, favour is according to what God sees fit, or what He deems is best, not what man thinks best or that may necessarily be approved by man. The favour of God comes with influence, it sets up connections.

In the Bible there are innumerable instances of God's favour and the favour of men. In this book we will be looking at some of these instances and how they relate to us individually, particularly the benefits that are attached to the favour of God, but also the dangers His favour may pose to us. My prayer and my advice to you is that, as you read this book, just as Paul wrote to members of the Church in Thessalonica, read it not as the word of man but as God's word, which is given to you because of His favour for you today. In other words, it is through God's favour that you are holding this book today, for this book is about to change your life. Paul said: "For this reason we also thank God without ceasing, because when you received the word of God which you heard from us, you welcomed it not *as* the word of men, but as it is in truth, the word of God, which also effectively works in you who believe." (1 Thessalonians 2:13)

In his letter to the Hebrews, the author said: "For indeed the gospel was preached to us as well as to them; but the word which they heard did not profit them, not being mixed with faith in those who heard it" (Hebrews 4:2, NKJV). My advice to you, therefore, is to allow your faith to merge with the words of this book so that your time spent reading it is beneficial.

Most important is the knowledge that this book brings: all believers are favoured. Just as the prophets warned, lack of knowledge has robbed many people of knowing God and walking in His favour: "my people are destroyed from lack of knowledge" (Hosea 4:6).

The Prophet Isaiah, too, lamented that the Israelites had been sent into exile or captivity because of their lack of knowledge. He said: "Therefore my people have gone into captivity, because *they have* no knowledge; their honourable men are famished, and their multitude dried up with thirst" (Isaiah 5:13). So you can see how important it is to acquire knowledge. When you lack knowledge as a favoured, blessed, and a free child of God, you will become captive. When you are in such a state of captivity it is easy to be subject to something or somebody that you are not supposed to become subjected to.

Failure to know who you are and what belongs to you is as bad as someone who does not have anything at all. With this book I will be removing the veil or ignorance from the face of many believers who are unaware that they possess one of the greatest assets, one that is part and parcel of the package of their salvation.

WHAT IS MEANT BY FAVOUR?

With both hands hanging above their heads one of the most song sing in churches today especially among Pentecostals is:

> **...*The favour of God is upon me oh***
> *The devil knows that I am a winner*
>
> *I am a winner*
> *I am a winner oh*
> *The devil knows that I am a winner*

I would like to believe without doubt that the song writer is trying to say that when you are favoured, you are also a winner. But the question I would like to ask is: Do these people singing this song really understand what favour means. Before I move further to discuss into details about favour let us first look at the meaning of favour

Favour can be described as:

- ✦ An act of kindness performed or granted to someone out of goodwill;

- ✦ A task somebody carries out for somebody else, e.g. to buy something for that person or to do something for that individual;

- ✦ It is also kindness, approval, partiality, friendly regard from a superior, or someone who is above the person to whom kindness is shown;

- ✦ It is to endow a person with spiritual blessing or special grace. It is a divine partiality, God's, or someone else's, who surpasses everybody in order to bless or to show kindness to someone;

- ✦ It is a special kindness or an opportunity given to someone even when in the eyes of everybody else he or she is not fit or qualified for this favour.

Favour and grace are interrelated, but have slightly different meanings: Grace, as we know, is the unmerited favour of God. That is, God doing something for someone, not necessarily because the person deserves it, but from His will as a result of His love for mankind. So I think grace has more to do with God's dealings with man; grace comes only through God. What I mean is this, that grace is an act of God and not an act of man; e.g. we are saved by His grace, that is salvation comes from God alone, for even when we were yet sinners, Paul said, Christ died for us (see Romans 5:8).

Favour, on the other hand, is most often given either by God himself—out of goodwill, by-passing everyone to do something for somebody even though the person does not deserve it nor has done anything to deserve it—or God Himself will cause someone, some person, to do something for another person out of goodwill even though the person may not deserve it. When someone under the influence of God shows special kindness, approval, partiality, or honour to someone who may not qualify – say someone in a superior position shows kindness to someone less important – this need not be because the person deserves special favour or because the person granting the favour even wants to show favour to this person, but because God is causing him/her to demonstrate this favour, even if in doing so the person may risk their job or even their life.

JESUS CHRIST: OUR ULTIMATE FAVOUR

Mary was favoured

There are seven recognised wonders in the world but, for me, none of these can be compared to the wonder or miracle of a virgin becoming pregnant, without knowing any man, by the Holy Spirit. Mary was highly favoured by God and her favour produced the greatest miracle of all time. Mary was a virgin who became pregnant without knowing any man. She gave birth to a Son, Jesus Christ, God's ultimate favour for mankind.

Key text: Luke 1:26–32

"Now in the sixth month the Angel Gabriel was sent by God to a city of Galilee named Nazareth, to a virgin betrothed to a man whose name was Joseph, of the house of David. The virgin's name *was* Mary. And having come in, the angel said to her, 'Rejoice, **highly favoured one**, the LORD *is* with you; blessed *are* you among women!' But when she saw *him*, she was troubled at his saying, and considered what manner of greeting this was. Then the angel said to her, 'Do not be afraid, Mary, for you have found *favour* with God. And behold, you will conceive in your womb and bring forth a Son, and shall call His name JESUS. He will be great, and will be called the Son of the Highest; and the LORD God will give Him the throne of His father David.'"

Here are some points selected from our key text above:

1. First of all the story is about the birth of Jesus foretold, predicted, or prophesied.

2. The reason the story begins with the statement: "Now in the sixth month …" is because it is a continuation of the story of Elizabeth and her husband Zechariah, the priest, about the prophecy of the birth of John the Baptist, their son, in Luke 1:5–25.

3. Verses 23–25 of that story read: "And so it was, as soon as the days of his service were completed, that he departed to his own house. Now after those days his wife Elizabeth conceived; and she hid herself five months, saying, 'Thus the LORD has dealt with me, in

the days when He looked on *me,* to take away my reproach among people.'"

4. The Angel Gabriel, whom God sent to Mary, was a top-ranking angel delivering top-ranking news, news that would change the course and the history of the whole world.

5. The woman at the centre of the story, receiving the news, is Mary. She is a virgin who has been given for marriage to a man called Joseph, but who has not had any intimate relationship with him.

6. The message that the Angel Gabriel delivers to Mary informs her that she is going to become pregnant with a Son by the Holy Spirit. She learns that her Son is to be called Jesus …

What do you make of the story as far as the theme of this book is concerned? In order to make something of the story, let us consider the following points:

We read that the Angel Gabriel was sent by God to a city in Galilee named Nazareth. Let us study Nazareth for a moment: it was Joseph and Mary's hometown. Nazareth was in Galilee in the northern part of Israel, a small town a long way from Jerusalem, which was the centre of Jewish life and worship. To assure ourselves that Nazareth was a very small and unknown town we can refer to what Nathanael said about Nazareth in John 1:45–46. Philip found Nathanael and said to him, "We have found Him of whom Moses in the law, and also the prophets, wrote – Jesus of Nazareth, the son of Joseph." And Nathanael said to him, "Can anything good come out of Nazareth?" Philip said to him, "Come and see." Nathanael's statement means that Nazareth was seen as a village from which nothing good could come.

I can also deduce from the narrative that Mary, the virgin at the centre of the story, was an ordinary girl from the village of Nazareth whose parents were not even known and are never even mentioned. But it was she who was chosen to be the mother of the Saviour of the whole world. She was chosen from among the many other girls and women of Israel, including the educated and those from cities such as Jerusalem, all because of **"God's Favour"**. This means that God, who always uses the ordinary things to accomplish extraordinary things, bypassed everyone in order to choose Mary for His great purpose.

The Angel Gabriel's greeting in verse 28–30 is yet further proof that it was God's favour that elevated Mary to such a prominent position, since many other women and virgins were denied. The scripture says: "And having come in, the angel said to her, 'Rejoice, **highly favoured one**, the LORD *is* with you; blessed *are* you among women!' But when she saw *him*, she was troubled at his saying this, and considered what manner of greeting this was. Then the angel said to her, 'Do not be afraid, Mary, for you have found *favour* with God.'"

In Luke 1:23–25 we learn from Elizabeth's statement that God's favour has the power to take away **reproaches, criticisms, or accusations**.

Studying Luke 1:23–32, the main point to make about this part of the Book is that the favour of God will find you wherever you are, even when you living are in obscurity and anonymity, even when you are buried in insignificance or unimportance; that is, when you are not known anywhere or when you are hidden as a result of the location you may come from, or due to the circumstances that surround you. What I am trying to get across to you is this: no matter what country or town you are from, regardless of the family you were born into, whether you are educated or uneducated like Elizabeth and Mary, or from Nazareth, which was just a small village at the time of the story, the favour of God will still locate you and bring you into the limelight, even if you are kept in the dungeon or overshadowed, no matter what thing or entity or person keeps you in obscurity. No matter what people think or say about you, God will find you for His favour. People may disqualify you, but the favour of God will always qualify you.

From the story of Elizabeth and Mary it is also clear that the favour of God will allow a woman to have children, no matter whether she is young or old. Mary, after all, was a virgin who had never had relations with any man, yet she became pregnant. This is something that had never happened before in the history of mankind. Thus we could say that her pregnancy was impossible. Elizabeth, on the other hand, even though in the Bible (Luke 1:6–7) it is said that she and her husband were righteous, yet we are informed they had not conceived a child because Elizabeth was barren. This means that she did not have God's blessing according to the Jewish tradition prevalent at that time. But in spite of Elizabeth's circumstances, the favour of God made way for her to have a child: this child was John the Baptist, the forerunner of our LORD Jesus Christ, for the favour of God always produces the best.

Another equally important part of this story is that when you are sure you are favoured you will always be thankful to the LORD.

When Mary received the information from the Angel Gabriel that she had found favour in God to become the mother of the Saviour of the world she could not hide her joy. First she went to Elizabeth and then she gave thanks to the LORD.

Mary's song of appreciation

"And Mary said: 'My soul glorifies the LORD and my spirit rejoices in God my Saviour, for he has been mindful of the humble state of his servant. From now on all generations will call me blessed, for the Mighty One has done great things for me—holy is his name. His mercy extends to those who fear him, from generation to generation. He has performed mighty deeds with his arm; he has scattered those who are proud in their inmost thoughts. He has brought down rulers from their thrones but has lifted up the humble. He has filled the hungry with good things but has sent the rich away empty. He has helped his servant Israel, remembering to be merciful to Abraham and his descendants for ever, even as he said to our fathers.' Mary stayed with Elizabeth for about three months and then returned home." (Luke 1:46–56)

Mary's song of appreciation is living testimony, as I said earlier, that Mary was an ordinary poor girl from the little town of Nazareth. Thank God for His favour in your life. Writing this book, the LORD has reminded me that people live in many different countries and hold many different positions. Some people are enjoying all manner of benefits; others are happily married to their partners, and some benefit from having a good job. Many, many situations and benefits, but all are the result of God's favour.

The LORD has reminded me also that many of us are out of His favour. This is because we fail to recognise and, therefore, appreciate His favour in our lives by giving Him thanks.

To conclude this section I pray that like Elizabeth, Mary, and the town of Nazareth, may the LORD open you to an understanding about what His favour can do for you. He may have done this for you already, so that you can be truly thankful to Him. Always remember that favour can turn any impossible situation like yours around.

The year of the LORD's favour

Key quotation: Isaiah 61:1–2

"The Spirit of the Sovereign LORD is on me, because the LORD has anointed me to preach good news to the poor. He has sent me to bind up the broken-hearted, to proclaim freedom for the captives, and release from darkness the prisoners, to proclaim the year of the LORD's favour and the day of vengeance of our God, to comfort all who mourn."

The quotation above is the prophecy of Isaiah about the Messiah, the Anointed One, and his transforming work under the power of the Holy Spirit.

This prophecy was fulfilled, according to Jesus in Luke 4:16–18, when Jesus was chosen to read the scripture in Nazareth. This was to establish his messianic credentials that the prophet had presented over 700 years before he was born.

In his writing, Luke said: "He went to Nazareth, where he had been brought up, and on the Sabbath day he went into the synagogue, as was his custom. And he stood up to read. The scroll of the Prophet Isaiah was handed to him. Unrolling it, he found the place where it is written: 'The Spirit of the LORD is on me, because he has anointed me to preach good news to the poor. He has sent me to proclaim freedom for the prisoners and recovery of sight for the blind, to release the oppressed, to proclaim the year of the LORD's favour.' Then he rolled up the scroll, gave it back to the attendant, and sat down. The eyes of everyone in the synagogue were fastened on him, and he began by saying to them, 'Today this scripture is fulfilled in your hearing.'" (Luke 4:16–21)

Focusing on the quotations from Isaiah and Luke above, and in light of the theme of this book, I want to bring your attention to what Jesus Christ is reiterating in verse 19 of Luke 4, which was first said by Isaiah in verse 2 of Isaiah 61, "The Spirit of the LORD is on me, because he has anointed me this day to proclaim to you the hour of the LORD's favour". Thus, as you hear me preach, teach, or as you read this book, the LORD's favour is with me.

Just as it was in the days of the Prophet Isaiah and in the days of Jesus Christ, so it is for us today. Many of us have been held captive by our mouths, or tongues, which is to say that we are held captive by what we speak about, even though we may be Christians. Through ignorance or lack of knowledge of God's word, and for many of us also because of our backgrounds and the way we have been brought up to believe and to act, our progress has been hindered. Many people are oppressed and in darkness; their progress hindered and joy suppressed by sicknesses and problems of many kinds.

But thank God for a time like this, where you and I have the opportunity to, as you read this book, transform your thinking through it. I believe I can announce to you, "The Year of the LORD's Favour", but that is only if we believe in our hearts that Jesus is LORD over our lives, and also declare this with our mouths, and truly believe that we are declaring the LORD's favour on us. The work of Jesus Christ, when he was here on Earth, fulfilled all that the prophet prophesied about him.

Jesus Christ, with this prophecy, was telling the people "I am the favour of God that you and everybody need; you've been waiting for the promised Messiah, the one who holds the freedom of the whole world."

The favour produces God's provision and healing

Further reading of Luke chapter 1:22–30 is yet another interesting part of the story, because this is the key quotation concerning God's favour, which brings provision and healing. I recommend that you read it in order to gain more understanding.

It is recorded that after Jesus had finished reading everyone spoke highly of him because of the power of the words that came out of his mouth. I take great interest in verses 25–27 when He (Jesus) said: "I assure you that there were many widows in Israel in Elijah's time, when the sky was shut for three and a half years and there was a severe famine throughout the land. Yet Elijah was not sent to any of them, but to a widow in Zarephath in the region of Sidon. And there were many in Israel with leprosy in the time of the Prophet Elisha, yet not one of them was cleansed—only Naaman the Syrian."

I know that favour, among many other meanings, also means that God's goodwill will bypass everyone in order to do something for somebody, even when the person does not deserve it. I know also that He (God) may cause a person to do something for another person out of goodwill, even though the person is undeserving of such favour or has done nothing to deserve it. This is to say that someone, under the influence of God, may show special kindness, approval, partiality, or honour to someone else who may be undeserving of such favour in the eyes of others.

So in this instance, for Jesus to mention the name of the widow in Zarephath and Naaman the Syrian, both of whom had done nothing to deserve what happened to them, I would like you, with me, to believe that it was only possible for the widow and her son to have enough to eat in the midst of famine, and for Naaman to be healed, because they received God's favour.

The story of the widow of Zarephath is told in 1 Kings 17:7–17.

Verse 8–9 says: "Then the word of the LORD came to him: 'Go at once to Zarephath in the region of Sidon and stay there. *I have directed a widow there to supply you with food.*'"

We know that God told the Prophet Elijah, "I have directed a widow there to supply you with food", which means that God was partial, he was selective, and chose the widow. He bypassed many people. Like the widow, in the midst of an economic crisis, when everyone is crying for money and other needs, God in His favour will supply all your needs knowing that when you are blessed you will take care of His servants or their work.

The story of Naaman, who was healed of leprosy, is also told in 2 Kings 5:1–14. Verses 1 and 14 respectively say:

Verse 1: "Now Naaman was commander of the army of the king of Aram. He was a great man in the sight of his master and highly regarded, because through him the LORD had given victory to Aram. He was a valiant soldier, **but** he had leprosy."

Verse 14: "So he went down and dipped himself in the Jordan seven times, as the man of God had told him, and his flesh was restored and became clean like that of a young boy."

As Jesus said, there were many leapers in Israel, not only Naaman, a Syrian, which indicates that God was partial to him.

In the statement, "He was a valiant soldier, **but** he had leprosy", the word "but" means that in spite of, after all his achievements, there was something wrong with him, he suffered from one of the deadliest diseases known at that time.

Furthermore, from Jesus' statement, "And there were many in Israel with leprosy in the time of the Prophet Elisha, yet not one of them was cleansed—only Naaman the Syrian", it is clear that God was partial to Naaman, who was not even an Israelite. I think I would be right in saying that God did this in order to say that He could be partial if he wanted to; that is, He can bypass everybody to meet your needs even though there may be many others who have the same needs as you.

Now, I wonder can you identify any "but" or any disability in your life as you listen to me preach, or while you are reading this book? I have good news for you, for no matter what "***but***", you too may benefit from the favour of God. He can remove any "but", no matter what country you come from or live in, and no matter what your background may be.

What I want you to understand from this story; what Jesus was trying to project through it is that He (Jesus) brought favour that was able to provide food in the midst of famine; favour that was able to bring healing to only one person even though there were many others who were sick. The favour of God in the context of Isaiah 61:1–2 and Luke 4:16–21 brings freedom to everyone who is prisoner or captive, either through lack of knowledge and faith, or through background, or through any demonic means. His favour is able to restore the sight of the blind and set the oppressed free.

The stories about the widow at Zarephath and Naaman the Syrian are also concerned with the fact that favour can be acquired or earned. This notion of acquiring or earning favour is treated in detail later in this book.

THE BENEFITS OF FAVOUR

When you are favoured you are shown favouritism or partiality by both God and man. Before we move on further, therefore, let us study favouritism or partiality a little.

Possibly you, like my little daughter, are wondering about this word jealousy. My young daughter once asked me a question when she heard that God was a jealous God. "Dad!" she said, "How could God be jealous, since jealousy is bad, and it is a sin?" If you are asking the same question about why God is partial, remember what the word says: "God does not show favouritism; God is no respecter of persons".

- ✦ Firstly, I want you to understand the quotation above in a different context.

✦ Secondly and importantly, God is sovereign, which means:

> He is self-determining, supreme, absolute, superior, He is in control of everything and everybody in the whole world. No one can advise Him or accuse Him of anything, no matter what He does; He chooses to do what He wants to do at any time.

✦ Thirdly, partiality or favouritism, like anger and jealousy, is not always to be considered as bad or sinful according to scriptures. This is what I would like to point out to you about anger and jealousy:

Anger: This is an act that is not always spoken of as sinful according to the scriptures, for even God is spoken of as being angry sometimes and Christ also displayed anger; yet Christians are warned against the possibility of sinning in anger. But this refers to anger that leads to sin, which is wrong, and is against God. Paul said: *"Be angry, and do not sin:* do not let the sun go down on your wrath" (Ephesians 4:26. Anger leads to bitterness, which does not only present danger to the person the anger is directed at, but is also damaging to the person that the anger is coming from.

Jealousy/envy: Again, like "anger", jealousy is not always spoken about as a sinful act according to the scriptures. This is an attitude of both God and man; it can be both positive and negative. In the positive sense, God is spoken of as being a jealous God, for He wants man to serve Him only: "You shall not bow down to them nor serve them. For I, the LORD your God, am a jealous God, visiting the iniquity of the fathers on the children to the third and fourth generations of those who hate Me." (Exodus 20:5). God is jealous when His children, instead of serving Him, begin to serve other gods.

Paul's jealousy for the Corinthian's Church

"For I am jealous for you with godly jealousy. For I have betrothed you to one husband that I may present you as a chaste virgin to Christ" (2 Corinthians 11:2)

Paul did not want what the Corinthian Church had, after all they were all sinners; rather he wanted them to devote their lives to God, much as it is expected that a man or woman devotes his or her love to their spouse. This is why Paul warned the Corinthians against sharing their love for the true doctrine with false doctrine.

The type of jealousy or envy that is sinful is the sort that develops against someone else because one feels that one should be in the position of the other person of whom one is jealous. This results in feelings of bitterness and unhappiness at someone else's position; or envy over their advantages, possessions, or maybe it presents as an overwhelming feeling of suspicion – for example, concerning a rival or competitor's influence, especially with regard to a loved one. The negative jealousy that leads to sin is a rage against God; take that of Joseph's brothers, for example, about which I will go into more detail later.

When you are favoured, you will be honoured by both God and man

The favour of God will take you to the palace; that is, you will be exalted to a highly respected position. There is more about this later in the book.

I remember a woman testifying in our church once, after I had preached about this message of favour. While I was preaching, having just said that the favour of God will take you to the palace, the woman shouted "Amen! I receive it in Jesus' name". About two months after this event, the young woman's school won an award and received an invitation to meet Her Majesty

Queen Elizabeth II. The woman had been chosen as one of only five students selected to meet her Majesty the Queen. You see, this woman had received favour from God. This favour took her to the Buckingham Palace, a place where she had never for a moment thought she would be invited, but the favour of God had made it possible.

In another incident, having heard me preach about what favour can do, another woman testified that she went shopping in a supermarket soon after she'd heard me. When she came to the till to pay for her shopping there was a long queue, but from nowhere the security guard, whom she had never met before, walked up to her and told her to move to the front of the queue, overtaking everybody. She was served before the many people who had been queuing before her, but none of them complained, even though she did not deserve to be treated in that manner since she was not elderly, pregnant, or disabled.

When you are favoured, that is, honoured by both God and man, you also receive special respect or gain a special reputation as stated in the scriptures.

"And the LORD gave the people *favour* in the sight of the Egyptians. Moreover the man Moses was very great in the land of Egypt, in the sight of Pharaoh's servants and in the sight of the people (Exodus 11:3).

The Bible says, in Proverbs 18:22 that a man is favoured by God when he finds a wife: "He who finds a wife finds what is good and receives favour from the LORD."

One day, while preaching about marriage, I remember telling my congregation about how this quotation (Proverbs 18:22) had been fulfilled in my own life. I told them that when I first met my wife and proposed to her I was very young, around 27 years old, and I had nothing; in fact, I was not even working because I had just finished studying at polytechnic. I was accepted by my future wife's parents without them considering my circumstances, however. Remember, this happened at a time when all parents are expecting a man's proposal to marry their daughters, but they are looking for someone who is highly educated, living and working in the city, or more so, someone who is from a wealthy background. However, irrespective of my poor background, and even though I was not even working at that time, I was accepted by my future wife's parents without question.

When I look back to those years and consider how God blessed me with such a wonderful woman; how she was given to me for marriage even though, as my wife told me later after we were married, she had received other proposals before mine, I can then only be truly grateful for the favour the Lord granted me in the sight of my wife's father. I say this to the glory of God, that the only asset, and in fact the greatest asset I had at that time, was Jesus, whom I have received as my Lord and Saviour, and who has changed my life.

My life, from the time I gave myself to Christ through to when I married, is living testimony of what God's favour can do to change a man. I can say with all confidence as Arch Bishop Benson Idahosa once said: "I am an example of a married Pastor, my marriage is worthy of emulation, when I preach or counsel people about marriage I do so with joy, passion and confidence as I can use my personal married life as an example to preach or advise others. I always tell those I counsel how blessed they are, because when I married many years ago I received no counsel or advice from anybody; Jesus through the Holy Spirit has been our counsellor even till now as we are still learning from him. I think at this point I am happy to tell you if you could commit your marriage to Him he will guard you too, and you will see the joy of marriage."

My wife has been the best thing that ever happened to me after my salvation, for the favour of God will always give you the best. She is my sister, mother, co-worker, and a friend, and between us the LORD has blessed us with three lovely children, Ben and Samuel, both princes, and our lovely princess Abigail.

- ✦ Favour will cause someone to show you kindness or select you for a position, even if they have to risk their life, position, or job;
- ✦ The favour of God brings promotion or exaltation;
- ✦ Favour will cause God and man to reveal to you things which are hidden from others;
- ✦ God's favour lasts longer than his anger the psalmist said: "For his anger lasts only a moment, but his *favour* lasts a lifetime; weeping may remain for a night, but rejoicing comes in the morning." (Psalms 30:5)

However, I want you to be aware that just as favour brings benefits it also presents dangers. That is to say that when you are favoured, you will attract hatred, hardship and troubles, of which some could even be life-threatening. Others may also be jealous of you; you may be envied by others. But the good news is that hardship doesn't mean you have lost God's favour.

The dangers of favour are discussed in more detail later in this book.

When the favour of God is upon you, whatever the evil planned against you, it will not succeed. Not only this powerful protection, but also that the evil which was planned against you will be reflected onto the person or people who were planning evil against you, for God protects those He favours.

Now in this world, I believe, where people are facing hatred and jealousy, lack of work, and many other problems, everyday and everywhere, I think one of the greatest commodities among believers is awareness of the need to pray. Even after salvation, and in the context of this book, I beseech you to pray and declare the LORD's favour everyday, in everything you do, and everywhere you go.

STORIES ABOUT THE BENEFITS AND THE DANGERS OF FAVOUR

Now let us look at some quotations and situations that relate to favour. We will consider both the benefits and the dangers that those involved encountered.

God's favour on Israel

The LORD chose Israel as his own, not because the Israelites were better than any other people on Earth, but out of His own love; out of His favour.

The LORD's favour on Israel stems from Genesis 12 when the LORD called Abraham, who was then called Abram, from among his own people, who were pagans, and promised to bless him and make him a great nation among all people.

In verses 1–3 we read: "The LORD had said to Abram, 'Go from your country, your people and your father's household to the land I will show you. I will make you into a great nation, and I will bless you; I will make your name great, and you will be a blessing. I will bless those who bless you, and whoever curses you I will curse; and all peoples on earth will be blessed through you.'"

God favoured Jacob

God showed favouritism or partiality to Jacob over his elder brother Esau. This is what the Bible has to say about the story: "Abraham became the father of Isaac, and Isaac was forty years old when he married Rebekah daughter of Bethuel the Aramean from Paddan Aram and sister of Laban the Aramean. Isaac prayed to the LORD on behalf of his wife, because she was barren. The LORD answered his prayer, and his wife Rebekah became pregnant. The babies jostled each other within her, and she said, 'Why is this happening to me?' So she went to enquire of the LORD. The LORD said to her, 'Two nations are in your womb, and two peoples from within you will be separated; one people will be stronger than the other, and the older will serve the younger.'" (Genesis 25:19–23)

Can anyone explain why God showed partiality to Jacob over his elder brother Esau? My answer is No!

Because God is Undisputable or unquestionable, He is Sovereign, the great "I AM" who does whatever pleases Him. The Favour of God is divine partiality, that is to say, it is partiality, but divine, and no one can explain or question why.

In the same way as told in the story of Esau and Jacob, I have witnessed God's divine partiality demonstrated many times; for instance, in many people who may possess gifts and talents from which they make their living. There are some people who may not have learnt some trades or who have not been trained to do certain things, yet they are well capable of doing them even more accurately than even those who are trained. Another divine favour or partiality is when someone is doing the same job as another person, let's say they are selling the same things that someone else is selling, and yet it is as if they are doing what they do on a different planet, because people seem to patronise their wares selectively. What this amounts to is divine partiality or favour from God.

Paul is alluding to this in the letter he wrote to the Roman Church when he comments on God's sovereign choice, his undisputed choice, and the partiality he showed to Jacob over his elder brother Esau. Read the whole of Romans, chapter 9 for more detail about this. In the context of this book, now let us read verses 11–14, where Paul said "(for *the children not yet being born, nor having done any good or evil, that the purpose of God according to election might stand, not of works but of Him who calls)*, it was said to her, '*The older shall serve the younger.*' As it is written, '*Jacob I have loved, but Esau I have hated.*' What shall we say then? *Is there* unrighteousness with God? Certainly not!"

Paul said, even before his children were born or had done anything good or evil, that God out of His sovereignty had chosen Jacob over his big brother. At the same time, the statement also means that Jacob had done nothing to deserve selection by God; nor had his big brother, Esau, done anything evil to deserve the lowly position God gave him to serve his younger brother. Paul asks in verse 14, "What shall we say then? Is there unrighteousness with God? Certainly not!" Why does Paul say "certainly not"? It is because God is holy and righteous and there is no unrighteousness in Him, for whatever He does is right. He never makes mistakes. So if He favours or blesses someone with anything, even though he passes over others to do so, it is because he is always right in everything he does and no one can complain.

Joseph was favoured by God

In Genesis 37:1–11 we are informed about Joseph and how because of the favour of God upon him, at age seventeen years, Joseph had a promising dream. In this dream, Joseph's father loved him more than any of his other brothers and also made him coat of many colours, which caused his other brothers to hate him. Joseph's brothers hated him all the more when he had his second dream, as the Bible says: "When he told his father as well as his brothers, his father rebuked him and said, 'What is this dream you had? Will your mother and I and your brothers actually come and bow down to the ground before you?'" (Genesis 37:10)

Before going any further allow me first to make a point and ask: do you believe that in the sight of men, for Jacob to love Joseph more than his other children and therefore make him coat of many colours, is wrong, because a father should not be selective among his children? But I would argue that Jacob's favour was not wrong, because the favour is God's doing, and anything in which God is involved cannot be wrong. The LORD was involved in Joseph's dream, because He showed Joseph the dream that told of his future life.

The second point I would like to make to you is this: to love one of your children more than the others is a risk you take; the result of this risk taken by Jacob was that Joseph was hated by his other brothers. I will discuss this point in more detail later.

Genesis 37:18–20 takes place sometime later, when Jacob sends Joseph to his brothers who are in the wilderness tending their father's sheep. They said to each other when they saw him coming, "let us kill him to see what comes of his dreams": "But they saw him in the distance, and before he reached them, they plotted to kill him. 'Here comes that dreamer!' they said to each other. 'Come now, let's kill him and throw him into one of these cisterns and say that a ferocious animal devoured him. Then we'll see what comes of his dreams.'"

Finally, Joseph's brothers put him into a pit and later sell him, while still enjoying the food he had brought them.

In Genesis 39:1–4 we also learn that the merchant who bought Joseph sold him on to Potiphar, an Egyptian, who was one of Pharaoh's officials. We then learn that because the LORD was with him, Joseph was favoured by his master Potiphar who put him in charge of everything he had.

Favour attracts many things including evil. In Genesis 39:6–20 the scripture records that Joseph was very attractive, and, just as it seemed that his problems were over, he found himself in even more serious trouble, because his master's wife had a crush on him and wanted him to go to bed with her, but he refused saying: "How then can I do this great wickedness, and sin against God?"

People frequently abuse favour when they are elevated to a higher position. They take advantage of their position and do all sorts of evil things. I have known and heard about many men who have neglected or divorced their wives for another woman because their present social position demands a more educated woman than the wife they married initially. In some cases their first wife was even part of their elevation process. There are others who may not want to even associate or talk to their life-long friends because now they consider themselves in the upper echelons of society. To deny people in this way is a very bad thing to do.

Back to Joseph's story: verses 11–12 say: "But it happened about this time, when Joseph went into the house to do his work, and none of the men of the house *was* inside, that she caught him by his garment, saying, 'Lie with me.' But he left his garment in her hand, and fled and ran outside."

Reading further into these verses one realises that Joseph fled leaving his garment in the hands of his master's wife, which she uses as evidence when, screaming for help, she puts a false charge on Joseph that he wanted to rape her (to use the modern term). The result for the innocent Joseph, who refused to sin, was that he was sent to prison.

Thank God, for once again, in the eyes of men, Joseph was in deep, deep trouble, and also it would seem he had finally lost sight of his dream. Yet Joseph was granted favour in the sight of the prison warder who, like Potiphar, put him in charge of the prison. Meanwhile, the enemy may well have thought that now it really was all over for Joseph, and they had managed to finish him off entirely. However, as verses 21–23 tell us: "But the LORD was with Joseph and showed him mercy, and He gave him *favour* in the sight of the keeper of the prison. And the keeper of the prison committed to Joseph's hand all the prisoners who *were* in the prison; whatever they did there, it was his doing. The keeper of the prison did not look into anything *that was* under *Joseph's* authority, because the LORD was with him; and whatever he did, the LORD made it prosper."

I want to point something out here concerning Joseph's life: it is both easy and right for someone to wonder how, if Joseph was favoured by God, why he successively found himself in trouble. I want also to emphasise that when you are favoured by God everything that happens to you - whether good or bad - is all part of God's divine plan for you, just as Joseph told his brothers when he revealed himself to them.

Finally, at the age of thirty, about thirteen years after his dream, the dream became reality when things started to go well for Joseph. Released from prison in order to interpret the king's dream, Joseph became Prime Minister, the second in command in Egypt, in a foreign land, after successfully interpreting the Pharaoh's dream. This is what the favour of God can do. His brothers thought they were murdering him to bury his dream (his favour), but in fact they were pushing him further into God's favour. Thirteen years after they had sold him, they bowed before him and referred to themselves and their father as "Joseph's servants", in fulfilment of the dream for which Joseph's father had rebuked him.

Genesis 43:26–28 records: "When Joseph came home, they presented to him the gifts they had brought into the house, and **they bowed down before him to the ground**. He asked them how they were, and then he said, 'How is your aged father you told me about? Is he still living?' They replied, 'Your **servant** our father is still alive and well.' **And they bowed low to pay him honour**."

Aren't these the very words Joseph's father used many years ago when, as an open-minded boy without any ill-feeling, Joseph told his family about his second dream and his father rebuked him? Genesis 37:10 says, "When he told his father as well as his brothers, his father rebuked him and said, 'What is this dream you had? Will your mother and I and your brothers actually come and bow down to the ground before you?'" May the LORD cause those who wish, or once wished, your death or downfall to bow down before you to pay you honour in Jesus' name for the favour that you were granted in order to get hold of a copy of this book.

I love Genesis 50:18–21, when it says that after their father died, due to their guilty conscience, Joseph's brothers were convinced that Joseph would pay them back for their treatment of him, putting him into the pit and selling him. The Bible says, "His brothers then came and threw themselves down before him. 'We are your slaves,' they said. But Joseph said to them, 'Don't be afraid. Am I in the place of God? You intended to harm me, but God intended it for good to accomplish what is now being done, the saving of many lives. So then, don't be afraid. I will provide for you and your children.' And he reassured them and spoke kindly to them."

Joseph's story is proof that no one has the power to wipe out God's favour from anybody's life. Others, out of jealousy, will be willing to kill you even as a favoured child of God, but what they don't realise is that no one can kill you, because you have God's favour. There is one exception: Abel was killed by his brother Cain because God looked on his sacrifice with favour. This I cannot explain, it is just one of those mysteries. God is sovereign, and no one can understand everything that He does or permits to happen. Deuteronomy 29:29 says: "The secret things belong to the LORD our God, but the things revealed belong to us and to our children forever, that we may follow all the words of this law."

To conclude this section I would like to say again by way of encouragement that, as a favoured child of God, when you face difficulties or challenges of any kind in life it does not mean you have lost God's favour. Whatever happens to you in life is part of God's divine plan for your life, for the favour of God is for a lifetime, as recorded by the psalmist: "For his anger lasts only a moment, but his favour lasts for a lifetime; weeping may stay for the night, but rejoicing comes in the morning" (Psalms 30:5). Here, the psalmist is saying that you may be weeping today because of an incident, whatever that may be, but the favour of God lasts for a lifetime. Your tears will be wiped away and give way to joy and the fruit of God's favour.

The story of Joseph is also living testimony that, when you are favoured whatever you do will be prosperous and all those around you will see the hand of God upon your life, whether or not those people around you believe in God. Even though Joseph was sold into slavery and imprisoned for a sin he did not even commit, he did not make to run away from it. And because wherever he was taken the favour of God followed him and, therefore, he prospered in everything he did, his masters saw this and put him in charge of everything.

Do not worry therefore when you are shown favour or preference, it is not your fault or your doing, for favour is orchestrated by God alone who knows the best, what, how, who, and when.

In Deuteronomy 7:6–8 Moses, the leader of the Israelites, told his people on their way to the Promised Land that the LORD had chosen them from among all nations of the Earth to be His treasured possession. This was not because they were more numerous than other peoples, in fact, as He said to them, they were the fewest of all peoples. The LORD favoured the Israelites because He loved them and wanted to keep the oath He swore to their ancestors that He would bring them out with a mighty hand and redeem them from the land of slavery, from the power of Pharaoh, the King of Egypt. His favour is able not only to lift the Israelites from slavery, but also to lift out anyone and everybody from any bondage.

Ruth is favoured

Out of God's favour, Ruth, a foreigner, became connected to the monarch of Israel, an ancestor of our LORD and Saviour Jesus Christ.

In Ruth 2:8–10 we read: "Then Boaz said to Ruth, 'You will listen, my daughter, will you not? Do not go to glean in another field, nor go from here, but stay close by my young women. Let your eyes be on the field which they reap, and go after them. Have I not commanded the young men not to touch you? And when you are thirsty, go to the vessels and drink from what the young men have drawn.' *So she fell on her face, bowed down to the ground, and said to him, 'Why have I found favour in your eyes, that you should take notice of me, since I am a foreigner?'"*

The story of Ruth, a Moabite woman who later became the wife of Boaz, a Jew, whose father was Salmon, a Jew, and his mother Rahab, the prostitute from Jericho, is an example and living testimony to the fact that favour recognises no foreigners; no matter who you are and where you come from your desire to seek the one and only true God will lead you to find Him, for he is not far away from any of us (from any nation) according to Luke in Acts 17:27.

In the context of this book I would like to reassure you that, no matter who you are or where you come from, your desire to seek the one and only true God will lead you to find Him, through His Son Jesus Christ, God's ultimate favour for mankind, and you will be favoured. When you receive Christ you receive favour as He *is* favour. This is also an endorsement to the fact that favour can be acquired or earned, a matter that I will treat in more detail later on in this book.

Find time to read the Book of Ruth, here you will discover a story that, like many other similar Books of the Bible, tells of a humble and hardworking woman, a Moabite from a pagan background, who knowing nothing but her determination to know the true God of the Israelites became connected to Him when she found Him, but the greatest thing of all is that when she found favour in the sight of Boaz, whom she later married, she became an ancestor of our Lord and Saviour Jesus Christ. I want you to hold on to the revelation I have just related to you, because favour will transform your life beyond your wildest dreams.

Ruth, a Moabite, a Gentile and a pagan, did not deserve to be anywhere near the family tree of our Lord and Saviour Jesus Christ, but she more or less became part of the monarchy of Israel. Only the favour of God is able to bring about such a transformation, only God's favour can make such a thing possible.

Let us consider what Ruth told Boaz in verse 10, after he had already told her all about the benefits he had been instructed to give her in verses 8 and 9 of Ruth, chapter 2.

Verse 10 says: "So she fell on her face, bowed down to the ground, and said to him, 'Why have I found *favour* in your eyes, that you should take notice of me, since I am a foreigner.'" Ruth acknowledges the fact that Boaz's recognition of her as a foreigner is only through favour. She knows that she is unworthy of such favour and knows she has done nothing to deserve the advantages accorded to her by Boaz since there were other, younger, Jewish women.

Ruth questions what she has done to deserve such kindness or favour especially when she comes from a different country, when she is a foreigner. To her mind, no one should be willing to show that sort of kindness to a foreigner, but what she did not know was that this favour was orchestrated by God, the author of promotion; that is, promotion comes from God. When God, out of His favour, is about to promote you, or causes anyone to show you kindness, nothing about you is considered, because His favour takes away any impediment.

I want you to take inspiration and a lesson from the words of Ruth, for whichever country you may be living in as a foreigner, as a believer and a righteous child of God, the favour of God that is upon your life knows no foreigners; in fact, you are a citizen of heaven, which is superior to any citizenship of any country on Earth. As a believer, you hold a passport to heaven, which qualifies you for everything, everywhere. Remember also that Joseph, a foreigner in Egypt, became Prime Minister of Egypt, and remember also that Daniel and his three

Hebrew friends were also honoured in a foreign land. No matter where you are, the favour of God can transform your life for the better. Just you believe it, claim it, and act like you know you are favoured by God, and you will experience favour in Jesus' name.

Ruth's Loyalty to Naomi

The book of Ruth is called the book of disloyalty, loyalty, and royalty.

It is interesting to note that in the heading for this part of book you can already see that the catch-word is Loyalty, this is because Ruth stayed loyal to Naomi, her mother-in-law, even after she wanted both Ruth and Orpah, her daughters-in-law, to return to their people following her decision to return to Bethlehem after the death of her husband and two sons, but Ruth in her determination to stay with her mother-in-law said:

> "Entreat me not to leave you, Or to turn back from following after you; for wherever you go, I will go; and wherever you lodge, I will lodge; your people *shall be* my people, **and your God, my God.**" (Ruth 1:16)

Secondly, unlike what many other people would have done, Ruth demonstrated yet more loyalty to her mother-in-law and lived with her even when things began going well for her in Bethlehem, until Naomi suggested to Ruth that she should think about finding a place of her own. Ruth 2:23–3:1 says: "So Ruth stayed close to the women of Boaz to glean until the barley and wheat harvests were finished. And she lived with her mother-in-law. One day Ruth's mother-in-law Naomi said to her, 'My daughter, I must find a home for you, where you will be well provided for.'"

Many people show how ungrateful they are by deserting the people who have helped them in times of difficulty. I have both witnessed and heard many stories where people have left home in dispute of those who have helped them to get a foothold in life. Some were brought from their native countries to other countries by their relatives or family members, others were sponsored to further their education or were given capital to start a business, but when the LORD blessed them through this help from others, these people yet turned against those who had been of help to them. But Ruth, at time when it looks like she was on familiar terms with the people and experiencing kindness from Boaz, still lived and served Naomi as her mother-in-law.

If anybody has helped you in life, in whatever way, never be ungrateful to them, but always remember their help by showing your appreciation to them. At the very least, buying them a card or present on occasions such as their birthday and Christmas will prove to them that you remember what they did for you.

Worst of all is when children – often out of immaturity and seeking to gain their freedom – fail to stay loyal to their parents even though their parents are able, at the right time, to find them a place to live. Some of these children, leaving abruptly, bring much hurt and discomfort to the parents, and, as a result, some of these parents in their pain and anguish say things that bring curses on their own children. If you are a child under your parents' umbrella and have been favoured to get hold of this book, I advise you never to hurt your parents by leaving home abruptly, no matter what happens. Wait until you receive your parents' blessing before you leave home. Waiting patiently for the right time like this will also offer you a way to return home any time you want should the need arise.

How Ruth became the wife of Boaz

In Ruth, chapter 3, the loyalty of the humble woman from Moab began to pay off when the old lady in her wisdom proposed a life-changing plan for Ruth. This plan would lead not only to someone providing for her, but also change the course of her destiny (3:2–4). In verse 5, Ruth promised to do exactly what her mother-in-law proposed.

Having followed every guideline given to her by Naomi her mother-in-law, verses 8–9 say: "In the middle of the night something startled the man; he turned—and there was a woman lying at his feet! 'Who are you?' he asked. 'I am your servant Ruth,' she said. 'Spread the corner of your garment over me, since you are a guardian-redeemer of our family.'"

Family-redeemer

First let's look at the word redeemer, which can mean saviour, rescuer, or liberator. Before moving on, allow me to explain to you what Ruth meant when she said "since you are a guardian-redeemer of our family", or family-redeemer. The word is first spoken to Ruth by Naomi in (Ruth 2:20).

Family-redeemer, according to the customs of Israel at the time when the story takes place, is a family member who willingly declares to take responsibility for a family member whose husband has died, and the woman agrees to marry one of the brothers of her dead husband, according to the Laws of Moses (Deuteronomy 25:5–10). In this Law of the family-redeemer, if the relative who is first in line to take this responsibility is not willing to do so then the responsibility is then handed to the second in line, if he is willing and able to take on the responsibility. The family-redeemer therefore redeems a widow from the grief of losing her husband as well as saving her from future difficulties by caring for her for the rest of her life.

Therefore when Ruth refers to Boaz as a family-redeemer she is saying that Boaz is the one who can save, rescue, or liberate her from the sorrow of losing her husband and also take care of her for the rest of her life.

Boaz, who had already shown kindness towards and had an interest in Ruth, and whose actions would be exemplary to any man, is delighted: In verse 10 we learn, "'The LORD bless you, my daughter,' he replied. 'This kindness is greater than that which you showed earlier: you have not run after the younger men, whether rich or poor.'" What Boaz says reminds me of a proverb that says: Advantage is like a mosquito that wants to go to the house of its mother-in-law when the wind blows and carries it into the house. I like what Boaz says to Ruth, "You have not run after the younger men, whether rich or poor", which I interpret as follows: Boaz, even though he was rich, understood very well that as Ruth was younger than him he would be unable to compete with men more youthful, so rightly, he commends Ruth for choosing him instead of the younger men.

Further reading reveals that with all Boaz's willingness and interest, even promising to do everything in his power to make Ruth honourable in the town, he noticed that there was big impediment that could turn out to be a big disadvantage: there was another man ahead of him in the line, who Boaz knew was more qualified as a family-redeemer than he was. Nevertheless, Boaz asks Ruth to stay for another night, thus that he might speak to the man who was the first in line with greater promise. In verse 13, Boaz tells Ruth: "Stay here for the night and in the morning if he wants to do his duty as your guardian-redeemer, good; let him redeem you. But if he is not willing, as surely as the LORD lives I will do it. Lie here until morning."

Ruth went back to her mother-in-law, Naomi, and told her everything that had happened. The old lady, in her wisdom, as ever encouraged Ruth not to worry, but to have patience and trust that all would be well.

Chapter 4 ends with an interesting story about how Boaz made every effort to gain the right to redeem Ruth and take her as his wife, but only after a roller-coaster decision by the first family-redeemer. In Verses 6–10 we read, "At this, the guardian-redeemer said 'Then I cannot redeem it because I might endanger my own estate. You redeem it yourself. I cannot do it.'" (Note that at this time in Israel, to legalise transactions and for the redemption and transfer of property to become final, one party took off his sandal and gave it to the other.) "Thus the guardian-redeemer said to Boaz, '"Buy it yourself.' And he removed his sandal. Then Boaz announced to the elders and all the people, 'Today you are witnesses that I have bought from Naomi all the property of Elimelek, Kilion, and Mahlon. I have also acquired Ruth the Moabite, Mahlon's widow, as my wife, in order to maintain the name of the dead with his property, so that his name will not disappear from among his family or from his hometown. Today you are witnesses!'"

When all the elders and all the other people present had declared they were witnesses, Boaz married Ruth.

How interesting it is to trace Ruth's journey, to see how she arrived at Boaz's field as an ordinary hardworking girl looking for work, so that she could earn something in return and preserve her own life and that of Naomi her mother-in-law, but how through favour she ends up becoming the owner of the field.

From verse 13 to the end of the chapter, the Bible records how Ruth is counted among the monarchs of Israel through the son she bore Boaz: "So Boaz took Ruth and she became his wife. When he made love to her, the LORD enabled her to conceive, and she gave birth to a son. The women said to Naomi: 'Praise be to the LORD, who this day has not left you without a guardian-redeemer. May he become famous throughout Israel! He will renew your life and sustain you in your old age. For your daughter-in-law, who loves you and who is better to you than seven sons, has given him birth.' Then Naomi took the child in her arms and cared for him. The women living there said, 'Naomi has a son!' And they named him Obed. He was the father of Jesse, the father of David."

The genealogy of David

"This, then, is the family line of Perez: Perez was the father of Hezron, Hezron the father of Ram, Ram the father of Amminadab, Amminadab the father of Nahshon, Nahshon the father of Salmon, Salmon the father of Boaz, Boaz the father of Obed, Obed the father of Jesse, and Jesse the father of David." (Ruth 4:13–22)

Through her loyalty and dedication Ruth, a Moabite woman, received favour that led her to be counted among the monarchs of Israel, God's chosen nation, as an ancestor of our LORD and Saviour Jesus Christ. Another interesting aspect of Ruth's story is that nothing was heard about her blood relatives afterwards; she is totally disconnected from the Moabite race and connected to the Jewish race instead, because she was redeemed by Boaz. It works the same way with believers: we are redeemed by Jesus Christ and so we are no longer connected to our former people or natural race; now we are connected to God through Christ Jesus, our ultimate favour from God. We are now the sons and daughters of God, Amen!

Thank God for Jesus Christ, a prototype of Boaz and our redeemer, who gave up all privileges as God and became a man, God's ultimate favour to redeem man from the guilt of sin and reconcile us to God. This is even when we had done nothing to deserve His favour, following Adam's loss of all the privileges the LORD had given him because of his disobedience.

In John 1:12–13, the Bible says: "But as many as received Him, to them He gave the right to become children of God, to those who believe in His name: who were born, not of blood, nor of the will of the flesh, nor of the will of man, but of God."

Writing to Titus, Paul assures us that we who were once like the ungodly have been saved by the kindness or the favour of God. He says: "At one time we too were foolish, disobedient, deceived, and enslaved by all kinds of passions and pleasures. We lived in malice and envy, being hated and hating one another. But when the kindness and love of God our Saviour appeared, he saved us, not because of righteous things we had done, but because of his mercy. He saved us through the washing of rebirth and renewal by the Holy Spirit" (Titus 3:3–5). Thank God for Jesus our redeemer. Halleluiah!

THE FAVOUR OF GOD BRINGS PROSPERITY

Many people, including some Christians, hate hearing the message of prosperity and do not even want to know about it, not at all. People who dislike this message generally criticise the churches and the ministers who preach about prosperity, and some members even leave their church because they think that the prosperity message is too often preached. But I believe that, when handled correctly, the prosperity message is good to hear, because as the message is about prospering, and the prosperity of man brings glory to God, surely therefore it is a good thing, a sign that a person has been blessed or is favoured by God. Thus I am happy in this part of the book and at this stage of my message to discuss the subject that favour brings wealth and that favour makes a man prosperous.

Israel had suffered at the hands of the Egyptians for over 400 years as slaves (Exodus 1), and when the time came for the Israelites to leave Egypt to go to the Promised Land, in fulfilment to the LORD's promise, the LORD promised to favour them in the sight of the Egyptians so that they would not leave empty handed.

First, in Exodus 3:21–22, the LORD said: "And I will give this people *favour* in the sight of the Egyptians; and it shall be that, when you go, you shall not go empty handed. But every woman shall ask of her neighbour, namely, of her who dwells near her house, articles of silver, articles of gold, and clothing; and you shall put them on your sons and on your daughters. So you shall plunder the Egyptians."

Secondly, in Exodus 11:1–3, the scripture says: "And the LORD said to Moses, 'I will bring yet one more plague on Pharaoh and on Egypt. Afterward he will let you go from here. When he lets you go, he will surely drive you out of here altogether. Speak now in the hearing of the people, and let every man ask from his neighbour and every woman from her neighbour, articles of silver and articles of gold.' And the LORD gave the people *favour* in the sight of the Egyptians. Moreover the man Moses was very great in the land of Egypt, in the sight of Pharaoh's servants and in the sight of the people."

The Israelites needed articles of silver, gold and clothing for their journey from Egypt, but not until God granted them favour in the sight of the Egyptians who would provide them with all the items they needed.

There are several useful points to note concerning this story:

- Israel, the Israelites, were about to leave Egypt under God's promise;
- These Israelites were poor slaves in Egypt;
- The good news was that their physical limitations did not limit the power of God;
- The LORD favoured them in the sight of the Egyptians who gave them everything they asked for. I see it as their wages dated back to over 400 years;
- The LORD tells them that they should ask for valuable things and the best of the land. In other words, the LORD is saying that they should be specific about what they ask for. This also means the LORD wants His children to desire the best.

Like the Israelites, we too, as children of God, may also need many things. However, like the Israelites, we may not qualify for what we need, or it may not be easy to attain what we need without the LORD's intervention, due to our status or the type of work we are doing.

But the good news is this: we serve a faithful God who always fulfils whatever He has promised, which is why He is trustworthy. God's promise to grant the Israelites favour was fulfilled in chapter 12, verse 36, where the Bible says: "And the LORD had given the people favour in the sight of the Egyptians, so that they [the Egyptians] granted them *what they requested*. Thus they plundered the Egyptians" (NKJV). The Israelites did not leave Egypt empty-handed; they left as the full beneficiaries, just as the LORD had promised.

To plunder means to rob a place or the people living there, or to steal goods using violence; this often also involves collateral damage, especially at times of war or civil unrest. In other words, you plunder or take things away from their rightful owners after you have won a victory in war; but the Israelites plundered the Egyptians and took away their valuables on request, not because they had won victory in a war or fight with the Egyptians, or plundered by force, but because God granted the Israelites favour in the eyes of the Egyptians. When you are favoured, you will lack nothing. Even things or positions that belong to your enemies or superiors will be given to you, if you specifically demand that this is so.

In the same way, as believers, we don't have to fight in order to benefit from the plunder, or to gain worth, because Jesus has already won the victory for us. It is up to us to go out and take what we will from the plunder through our faith. I pray and release to you whatever you have worked for over the years, whatever your enemies have taken away from you and even from your ancestors, I pray through the favour of God (Jesus Christ) that it will be given to you as your rightful possession.

THE FAVOUR OF GOD BRINGS REVELATION

The favour will make God or men reveal to you what has previously been concealed from others. We witness this in the story told below, in which God reveals his plans to Abraham, first about Abraham himself, and then about his intention for Sodom and Gomorrah. This was because Abraham had favour with God.

First in Genesis 18, verse 3 Abraham says, "If I have found favour in your eyes, my LORD, do not pass your servant by."

Further reading shows that the angels of the LORD accepted Abraham's invitation as a result of God's favour. After spending some time and having dinner with him, the LORD revealed His plan for Abraham first.

Genesis 18, verse 10 says, "Then one of them said, 'I will surely return to you about this time next year, and Sarah your wife will have a son.' Now Sarah was listening at the entrance to the tent, which was behind him."

Secondly, the Lord then reveals to Abraham his plans for Sodom and Gomorrah.

In verses 16–17 of the same chapter we read: "When the men got up to leave, they looked down toward Sodom, and Abraham walked along with them to see them on their way. Then the Lord said, 'Shall I hide from Abraham what I am about to do?'"

Reading to the end of the chapter, we see Abraham interceding for the righteous, which provides further evidence that the Lord never destroys the unrighteous together with the righteous. I pray that as you read this book the Lord will open your eyes to the purpose of your life and that He will even reveal the plans of your enemies, so that they cannot outwit you, as Paul said, "... in order that Satan might not outwit us. For we are not unaware of his schemes." (2 Corinthians 2:11)

Samuel gained favour from God

"And the boy Samuel continued to grow in stature and in favour with the LORD and with men." (1 Samuel 2:26)

As a result of God's favour, God revealed to Samuel His secret plans, even though Samuel was very young to know the voice of God. Out of God's favour, it was Samuel who was chosen by God to succeed Eli as a priest, instead of Eli's children, who were in direct line. Not only did Samuel become a priest, but he was also a prophet and a judge; he held three positions or offices. You can find out more about Samuel when you read 1 Samuel, but in the context of this part of the book, let us consider how God will reveal to you, or cause others to reveal to you, what has been concealed from others.

We read in 1 Samuel 3:11–14: "And the LORD said to Samuel: 'See, I am about to do something in Israel that will make the ears of everyone who hears of it tingle. At that time I will carry out against Eli everything I spoke against his family—from beginning to end. For I told him that I would judge his family for ever because of the sin he knew about; his sons made themselves contemptible and he failed to restrain them. Therefore,

I swore to the house of Eli, "The guilt of Eli's house will never be atoned for by sacrifice or offering.""'

In the quotation above, see how the LORD revealed to the young Samuel something that not even his master Eli, his children, or any Israelite knew, because God favoured him. How would you feel, and what would you think, if you were the young Samuel who was chosen by God to reveal something about which no one around you has any idea? This is what favour can give you.

My personal testimony on favour

I think this is the right and the good time to share a personal testimony with you. This is a testimony about my former boss, Andrew, and the favour he showed me when he sold his factory, where I was working at the time. One day Andrew called me to his office and told me secretly, without telling any of the other members of staff, that he had sold the business. He not only told me this, even though I was the only person of my nationality among the workers who were otherwise predominantly Greek like Andrew, but also paid me my wages while he did not pay the others. On top of revealing to me alone that he had sold the business to someone else, he also asked me to tell him how much I wanted as wages; apparently the man who was taking over the business had asked Andrew to tell him how much he paid all of his employees so that he could continue to pay us the same salary. Giving me this opportunity, and knowing that I had found favour in his sight, I spoke to him confidently. I told Andrew how much I wanted to be paid, which was more than I had been receiving before, and this is the sum Andrew told my new boss I had been receiving as wages. Without doubt, this story demonstrates the favour of God. Praise God! Interestingly, after Andrew had gone and the new boss had been running the factory for some weeks, all the other staff were still mourning their lost wages. In fact, to prevent anyone knowing that Andrew had favoured me and I had been paid, I had to join the masses and sing the same chorus.

THE FAVOUR OF GOD WILL TAKE YOU TO THE PALACE

The favour of God will take you to where you are not qualified to be. In fact, in the context of this book, it will take you to the palace, the place of the highest esteem and a position of the highest honour.

God's favour on Moses as a little boy

I would like you to believe with me that it was God's favour that preserved the life of little Moses after the Pharaoh ordered the slaughter of all male Hebrew children; it was also the favour of God that prevented Moses drowning in the River Nile. Moses floated down the river in a basket among the reeds without any harm coming to him from predators, such as fish, or any other dangerous reptile or land-based animal.

I also enjoy the divine appointment that God made between the little boy and the Pharaoh's daughter. The Bible tells us that the Pharaoh's daughter went down to the River Nile to bathe, and that, here, she and her attendants were walking along the riverbank. She saw the basket among the reeds and sent her female slave to get it. She opened it and saw the baby. He was crying, and she felt sorry for him. "'This is one of the Hebrew babies,' she said. Then Moses' sister appears and asks the Pharaoh's daughter, 'Shall I go and get one of the Hebrew women to nurse the baby for you?' 'Yes, go,' she answered. So the girl went and got the baby's mother. Pharaoh's daughter said to her, 'Take this baby and nurse him for me, and I will pay you.' So the woman took the baby and nursed him." (Exodus 2:5–9)

What a privilege favour is! While other Hebrew children were being slaughtered, Moses was not only enjoying the favour of God, but also the favour of the Pharaoh's daughter. She knew that Moses was among the Hebrew children who were supposed to be killed, and yet the Pharaoh's daughter showed compassion for the child and instantly chose him to be her son. She agreed to Moses' sister Miriam's suggestion to ask a Hebrew mother to nurse the child, and so Miriam asks her own mother. Moses' mother is then paid to nurse her own son, who is supposed to have perished with the other Hebrew children. God's favour brings protection and will keep you safe from any law; God's favour can even preserve your life.

To conclude this section, I would like to share with you once again what favour can do, this time in the context of Moses' story. Moses, who later would become the deliverer of the Israelites from slavery at the hands of the Egyptians, was brought up, trained, and educated in the house of Pharaoh for forty years. This means that he was acquainted with all Egyptian traditions, customs, and every secret, as he had been brought up in the camp of his enemies. This was only possible through the favour of God. Is it not interesting to realise that the very man who issued the edict to slaughter all Hebrew children throughout his homeland was also training the very person who was going to be the deliverer of those people? What a God we serve when through His favour He can do such a wonderful thing!

✦ David was favoured by God

In 1 Samuel, chapters 8–10, we are informed that the Israelites wanted a king. Even though their request displeased God, He yet gave them a king in the person of Saul, the first King of Israel. However, in chapters 13 and 15 we are informed of Saul's disobedience; it is because of his disobedience that God rejects Saul as king. Then God seeks for Himself another man to succeed Saul as king, to rule over His people.

"'You have done a foolish thing,' Samuel said. 'You have not kept the command the LORD your God gave you; if you had, he would have established your kingdom over Israel for all time. But now your kingdom will not endure; the LORD has sought out a man after his own heart and appointed him ruler of his people, because you have not kept the LORD's command.'" (1 Samuel 13:13–14)

The story above concerns Israel at a time when it was warring with the Philistines, the Israelites' arch enemy at the time. To guarantee victory, however, Israel had to offer sacrifice to the LORD. Saul offered the sacrifice instead of waiting for Samuel, who as priest was responsible for offering the sacrifice, and which he had promised to do according to the Law (Deuteronomy 12:5–14).

When Samuel arrived he exclaimed: "'Does the LORD delight in burnt offerings and sacrifices as much as in obeying the LORD? To obey is better than sacrifice, and to heed is better than the fat of rams. For rebellion is like the sin of divination, and arrogance like the evil of idolatry. Because you have rejected the word of the LORD, he has rejected you as king.'" (1 Samuel 15:22–23)

Saul, once again out of disobedience, had spared the life of the king of the Amalekites, and some animals, which according to the Law were supposed to be used for sacrifice to the LORD. This was in addition to ignoring the instructions Samuel the priest had given him as directed by God in 1 Samuel 15:1–3: "Samuel said to Saul, 'I am the one the LORD sent to anoint you king over his people Israel; so listen now to the message from the LORD. This is what the LORD Almighty says: "I will punish the Amalekites for what they did to Israel when they waylaid them as they came up from Egypt. Now go, attack the Amalekites and totally destroy all that belongs to them. Do not spare them; put to death men and women, children and infants, cattle and sheep, camels and donkeys."'"

Now, out of His favour, God chose David, a simple shepherd boy and the youngest son of Jesse, whose mother even the Bible does not record. God chose David ahead of his elder brothers to be the King of Israel after he had rejected King Saul. From 1 Samuel

16:6–13, it becomes clear that the favour of God bypasses any outward appearance, for this is how man judges things. What men see with their eyes can either qualify or disqualify a person for a position, as the Prophet Samuel did in the house of Jesse, but God judges according to his favour even when the chosen one may have done nothing to deserve the right or position bestowed on him or her.

Verses 6–7 say: "So it was, when they came, that he looked at Eliab and said, 'Surely, the LORD's anointed *is* before Him.' But the LORD said to Samuel, 'Do not look at his appearance or at the height of his stature, because I have refused him. For *the* LORD *does* not *see* as man sees; for man looks at the outward appearance, but the LORD looks at the heart.'"

Samuel's perception of the rest of Jesse's sons, who were paraded before him as Jesse called them up one by one, was the same as his perception of Eliab, but the LORD rejected them one by one, as He had the first, until all of them had been called up and rejected. Realizing that the LORD had rejected all of them, Samuel asked Jesse if there were any other sons left, to which Jesse replied: "'There remains yet the youngest, and there he is, keeping the sheep.' Samuel said none of us will sit down until he is here. When David has been brought down Samuel took the horn of oil and anointed him in the midst of his brothers; and the Spirit of the LORD came upon David from that day forward. So Samuel arose and went to Ramah."

What I am saying here is this: David was chosen to become the second King of Israel because he was the beneficiary of God's favour. David surpassed each one of his older brothers and was elevated to a place of honour. From a humble shepherd, David is elevated to the highest position of the land, the King of Israel, even though men, including his own father, had disqualified him. David's father, Jesse, had not even invited his youngest son to join his brothers when Samuel requested that Jesse call his sons to what I call the "identity parade". Again, allow me to remind you that the favour of God transcends the minds of men and sees beyond the eyes of men.

Men may look at outward appearance and judge and disqualify you, but the LORD looks at the heart; do not, therefore, worry about what men may say or think of you; what God says about you is all that matters. That which carries weight for what God proposes cannot be deposed but, on other hand, as the Bible (Proverbs 19:21) says "Many are the things in the heart of man although only the will of God shall prevail."

It is for this reason that Jesus warns his listeners in John 7:24, saying: "Do not judge according to appearance, but judge with righteous judgment." (NKJV)

Alternatively the (NIV) says: "Stop judging by mere appearances, but instead judge correctly." Therefore, it is not what you see; think and, therefore, judge by what God has approved.

To conclude this section, let me reiterate: it does not matter whether you are less well educated than others, whether you are the youngest among many, or married or single. No matter your situation, notice that promotion comes from the LORD, as the psalmist said: "For exaltation comes neither from the east nor from the west nor from the south. But God is the Judge: he puts down one, and exalts another." (Psalms 75:6–7)

If God out of his favour exalted David, a lowly shepherd boy, to the position of the King of Israel he will do the same for you as a favoured child (a believer).

I encourage you therefore never to be discouraged because of what men think or say about you. Remember that God is the only righteous judge and that He always chooses and uses the ordinary things and ordinary people to accomplish extraordinary things. Through His favour, which is in His son Jesus Christ, He sees that you are fit for every good thing. Let men say what they want and think what they want, for the bottom line is that your future is not in the hands of men, but in the hands of God. As Ephesians 2:10 says: "For we are His workmanship, created in Christ Jesus for good works, which God prepared beforehand that we should walk in them."

✦ King David favoured Mephibosheth

When David became the King of Israel he also, just as the LORD had done for him, showed kindness or favour to some individuals who maybe did not deserve it nor had ever done anything to deserve the favour accorded to them.

The story of David is told in 2 Samuel 9:1–13. Let us for now reflect on verses 1–3: "David asked, 'Is there anyone still left of the house of Saul to whom I can show kindness for Jonathan's sake?' Now there was a servant of Saul's household named Ziba. They called him to appear before David, and the king said to him, 'Are you Ziba?' 'Your servant,' he replied. The king asked, 'Is there no-one still left of the house of Saul to whom I can show God's kindness?' Ziba answered the king, 'There is still a son of Jonathan; he is crippled in both feet.'"

But before I discuss further the details about this person called Mephibosheth and what had been accorded to him because he was favoured, I would first like to introduce the four important personalities who populate this story in 2 Samuel, chapter 9. These individuals are:

> Saul: The first King of Israel (1 Samuel 8–10), the father of Jonathan;

> David: the second King of Israel, the king at the centre of the story, who wanted to grant favour;

> Jonathan: the eldest son of King Saul and a friend of David;

> Mephibosheth: the son of Jonathan and the grandson of King Saul, the man who was about to receive favour.

The Bible tells us that David asks, "'Is there anyone still left of the house of Saul to whom I can show kindness or favour for Jonathan's sake?' (2 Samuel 9:1). For more information about the background of Saul and how he was chosen by God and anointed as the first King of Israel, and to read more about David, please refer back to the text above under the heading "The favour of God will take you to the palace".

A brief commentary on David and Jonathan's relationship/friendship

In 1 Samuel 17 it is recorded that, as result of David's remarkable work in killing the Philistine giant Goliath, he was taken to the palace to meet King Saul who wanted to talk to him about his exploits and learn about whose son he was.

In Samuel 18:1–4 we read: "Now when he had finished speaking to Saul, the soul of Jonathan was knit to the soul of David, and Jonathan loved him as his own soul. Saul took him that day, and would not let him go home to his father's house anymore. **Then Jonathan and David made a covenant, because he loved him as his own soul.** And Jonathan took off the robe that *was* on him and gave it to David, with his armour, even to his sword and his bow and his belt." (NKJV) What a demonstration of love this is.

The relationship between David and Jonathan was so strong that even when King Saul, who was Jonathan's father tries to kill David, Jonathan exposes the plot to David. Jonathan also speaks highly of David to his father (1 Samuel 19:1–4).

David proved his love in his words when he heard of Jonathan's death:

When David heard of Jonathan's death he laments, saying:

"I grieve for you, Jonathan my brother; you were very dear to me. Your love for me was wonderful, more wonderful than that of women." (2 Samuel 1:26)

"I am distressed for you, my brother Jonathan; you have been very pleasant to me; your love to me was wonderful, surpassing the love of women." (2 Samuel 1:26)

These are the words of David when he heard of his dear friend Jonathan's death. I wonder how many of us could say this today, even in response to a similar situation concerning our spouse, let alone a friend. This, to me, is the demonstration of true love for a friend to the highest degree.

Brief details about Mephibosheth

In response to David's question in 2 Samuel 9:1, verse 2 informs us that Ziba, a servant in Saul's house, says that only one son of Jonathan's is still alive, and he is crippled in both feet. Later verses indicate that this son of Jonathan's is called Mephibosheth.

The reason Mephibosheth was the only son alive

Jonathan died with his father and two brothers in Gilboa. "Now the Philistines fought against Israel; the Israelites fled before them, and many fell slain on Mount Gilboa. The Philistines pressed hard after Saul and his sons, and they killed his sons Jonathan, Abinadab, and Malki-Shua. The fighting grew fierce around Saul, and when the archers overtook him, they wounded him critically." (1 Samuel 31:1–3)

"The next day, when the Philistines came to strip the dead, they found Saul and his three sons fallen on Mount Gilboa." (1 Sam 31:8)

The story of the death of Saul and his three sons is also recorded in 1 Chronicles 10:1-22.

Thank God for His favour that I have stood on the mountain where Saul and his three sons died and also visited Beth Shan, where their bodies were taken, by the Philistines, and hanged at the city wall and many other places. On two occasions when I have been given the opportunity to visit Israel, the Promised Land, I did not feel that I was deserving of this great opportunity: what had I done to deserve to be in a place that, when I was younger, I believed was not on this planet Earth? Praise the name of the LORD for allowing me the opportunity to visit this and many other remarkable sites in the Holy Land.

How Mephibosheth, Jonathan's son, came to be lame or crippled

"Jonathan son of Saul had a son who was lame in both feet. He was five years old when the news about Saul and Jonathan came from Jezreel. His nurse picked him up and fled, but as she hurried to leave, he fell and became crippled. His name was Mephibosheth." (2 Samuel 4:4)

In retelling this interesting story, you may relate it to your life: before I go any further, therefore, I would like to say to you that, like Mephibosheth, you too may have been left alone for whatever reason; but as I have said before, when God's favour comes, in other words when you are favoured either by God or by man, it does not matter where you are or what your present situation may be, for you will be exalted to a place of high esteem, a place above your wildest dreams, for the favour of God knows no bounds, transcends any barriers, no matter what the situation.

From the story about Mephibosheth, we may note how the boy became lame in both feet and, also, how he describes himself to the king. He tells the king that he is nothing in the eyes of men; as he bowed down, he said, "What is your servant, that you should notice a dead dog like me? Who am I?" (2 Samuel 9:8)

As we know, live dogs eat the crumbs of food that fall to the ground from their master's table. In this case, however, because of his situation, Mephibosheth likened himself to a "dead dog", and a dead dog is not even qualified to scavenge the crumbs that fall from his master's table because it is dead. But the good news is that favour elevated Mephibosheth to the palace; he finds himself eating at the same table as the king, a man in the highest position in the land. The favour of God will do the same for you, if you believe. Say Amen to that!

In 2 Samuel 9:10–11, the king's favour commands that Ziba and his fifteen sons become servants of Mephibosheth. "You and your sons and your servants are to farm the land for him and bring in the crops, so that your master's grandson may be provided for. And Mephibosheth, grandson of your master, will always eat at my table (now Ziba had fifteen sons and twenty servants). Then Ziba said to the king, 'Your servant will do whatever my Lord the king commands his servant to do.' So Mephibosheth ate at David's table like one of the king's sons."

Like Mephibosheth, you too may be lame, meaning that you are disabled, and maybe you feel inadequate and ineffectual in life; in fact, you may feel that you are counted as useless, lesser among the garbage; you may feel that, in the words of Mephibosheth, you are nothing but a "dead dog". But, irrespective of how you see yourself or how others see you, I am here to announce to you that by reason of God's favour you, too, will be elevated to a place of dignity, you will be dining with great men as well. Even though you may feel that you are not respected by anyone, you will be respected. And those you have been serving will become your servants, like Ziba and his sons, who became the servants of Mephibosheth.

You may look back on the life that you began a very long time ago. You may look back with regret: even though you are not lazy and have tried all means to make something of your life, having done all sorts of jobs, still you have not progressed and feel you have nothing to show for your toil. This is all because you've been made lame or been crippled in life, for example, financially always needing or never gaining a promotion. Wherever you are stuck in life, I decree and declare movement, a shift in your life, by reason of the LORD's favour.

Another interesting connection to make from Mephibosheth's story of transformation is that the favour of God can also change your location or environment. From Lo Debar, Mephibosheth was transported and relocated to live in Jerusalem, the city of David, and the capital of Israel.

Importantly, Lo Debar, the town that Mephibosheth came from, is usually believed to be the same as Debir, the homeland of the Tribe of Gad (Joshua 13:26). The word Debir means "without pasture" (2 Samuel 17:27), "no word", or "no communication". I refer to this, therefore, because I would like to mention that for Mephibosheth to be from Lo Debar means that he was in a place of no contact and no consultation. This suggests a place in which one cannot talk to anyone or exchange ideas through means of a letter, telephone call, fax, or email. That Lo Debar/Debir also means "no pasture" suggests that it was a place where it was difficult to survive, where there was little to eat; a place of the highest degree of poverty.

In conclusion, allow me to repeat my assurance to you in light of Mephibosheth, who in spite of coming from Lo debar, still received the favour of God through David. Mephibosheth's life changed when he was taken to Jerusalem and, by reason of the same favour of God, your location will also change for the better if you believe in Him. You will be relocated from your village where no man knows you, where even sustenance has become a problem, and be exalted to a place beyond your wildest dreams. You will become connected to the rest of the world, and even more opportunities will become accessible to you. This is because the favour of God brings change and sets up connections. God's favour will even speak for you in your absence.

✦ Solomon is favoured

Out of God's favour, Solomon was chosen to succeed his father as the King of Israel ahead of his older brothers, who were all fighting for the throne; Absalom wanted the position so much that he was even willing to kill his own father, David, to take the throne (2 Samuel 15).

David's fourth son, Adonijah (2 Samuel 3:4), also put himself forward for the position as the scriptures record: "Now Adonijah, whose mother was Haggith, put himself forward and said, 'I will be king.' So he got chariots and horses ready, with fifty men to run ahead of him." (1 Kings 1:5, NIV)

It was Solomon – even though he had done nothing to deserve the position – who was chosen, because God's favour brought him elevation. I am reminded of the sentiments of two proverbs told by the elders:

The owner of something is the person who must consume or make use of it, not the person who desires or longs for it.

If you are not created king, even if you put on a crown, no one will recognise or admire you.

You see, all the efforts of Solomon's older brothers were in vain, because God had other plans.

David chose Solomon as his successor to the throne

"Then King David said, 'Call in Bathsheba.' So she came into the king's presence and stood before him. The king then took an oath: 'As surely as the LORD lives, who has delivered me out of every trouble, I will surely carry out this very day what I swore to you by the LORD, the God of Israel: Solomon your son shall be king after me, and he will sit on my throne in my place.' Then Bathsheba bowed down with her face to the ground, prostrating herself before the king, and said, 'May my lord King David live forever!'" (1 Kings 1:28–31)

In support of Solomon's selection, the whole city shouted with joy

"From there they have gone up cheering, and the city resounds with it. That's the noise you hear. Moreover, Solomon has taken his seat on the royal throne." (1 Kings 1:44–46)

Even Adonijah, one of Solomon's older brothers, confirms that Solomon has been chosen by God. Remember that Adonijah had previously pronounced himself king, so now he had to show humility in order to pronounce: "'As you know,' he said, 'the kingdom was mine. All Israel looked to me as their king. But things changed, and the kingdom has gone to my brother; for it has come to him from the LORD.'" (1 Kings 2:15)

David informs his son Solomon that he is going to build the LORD's Temple

David had longed to build a temple for the Lord, but his desire was rejected by God, who told him that the Temple would be built by his son Solomon: "Then he called for his son Solomon and charged him to build a house for the LORD, the God of Israel. David said to Solomon: 'My son, **Lord** I had it in my heart to build a house for the Name of the LORD my God. But this word of the LORD came to me: "You have shed much blood and have fought many wars. You are not to build a house for my Name, because you have shed much blood on the earth in my sight. But you will have a son who will be a man of peace and rest, and I will give him rest from all his enemies on every side. His name will be Solomon, and I will grant Israel peace and quiet during his reign. He is the one who will build a house for my Name. He will be my son, and I will be his father. And I will establish the throne of his kingdom over Israel forever."'" (1 Chronicles 22:6–10)

Unfortunately, maybe out of insecurity, when he became king, Solomon ordered the killing of his brother Adonijah. Insecurity can cause one to do terrible things; it can even lead to murder: "'Now therefore, *as* the LORD lives, who has confirmed me and set me on the throne of David my father, and who has established a house for me, as He promised, Adonijah shall be put to death today!' So King Solomon sent by the hand of Benaiah the son of Jehoiada; and he struck him down, and he died." (1 Kings 2:24–25, NKJV)

For more discussion about the effects of insecurity, please watch out for my upcoming book entitled *Insecurity*.

Solomon's story is yet another example of God's favour at work. Solomon, like his father, was chosen and anointed ahead of his older brothers to succeed his father as the third King of Israel, irrespective of the background of his parents' marriage (2 Samuel 11 and 12). This is a predicament that interests me enormously, and now I would like to share with you some elements of this situation.

It is obvious that Solomon would have been disqualified by all men, even all of us, were we asked. However, Solomon was chosen by his father and supported by

God and all the people, which can be understood only as an act of God's favour.

In 2 Samuel 12:24–25 we read: "Then David comforted his wife Bathsheba, and he went to her and made love to her. She gave birth to a son, and they named him Solomon. The LORD loved him; and because the LORD loved him, he sent word through the Prophet Nathan to name him Jedidiah. The name Jedidiah means 'the LORD's darling.'"

In the context of this book, concerning the fact that Solomon was chosen to be King, what I wish to project to you is that the favour of God will supersede anything to do with your background, however lowly, and elevate you to the throne of your life.

Solomon's story, like all the other stories about how the favour of God will elevate men to the palace, means that promotion comes from God not from man. As the psalmist tells us, "Do not lift up your horn on high; do *not* speak with a stiff neck. For exaltation comes neither from the east nor from the west nor from the south. But God *is* the Judge: He puts down one, and exalts another." (Psalms 75:5–7, NKJV)

God decides who deserves to be promoted not men. If promotion came from men many of us would not be where we are now. I will offer you more personal testimony later on in this book, but, until then, I want to beseech you to never write yourself off, never write off anything in life, even when some people may see you as a loser. Always know that your future or destiny is determined by God and not by men: He has control over all things and that includes your life. Men, even those close to you, will always wish your downfall. They will be saying or doing things to discourage you as you try to move forward in life, but I challenge you not to give in, for if you trust in God your future success is always guaranteed.

✦ Esther became queen as a result of God's favour

Esther's story provides three different aspects relating to favour, the theme of this book:

1. Esther was selected to become queen in a foreign land as a result of God's favour;

2. Because of God's favour, Esther and her people, the Jews, attracted jealousy and hatred, which meant that their lives were threatened by Haman. More about the dangers of favour later in this book;

3. God's favour brought prosperity and elevation to Mordecai, Esther's uncle.

I will highlight each of these points as the story unfolds below:

In Esther, chapter 1 we are informed about the days of King Xerxes, the fifth King of Persia. Persia, which was an ancient kingdom within the modern-day province Iran, was the dominant kingdom in the Middle East after the fall of Babylon (in 539 BCE) and was ruled from the fortress city of Susa. Persia held about 127 principalities that stretched from India to Ethiopia.

It is said that, in the third year of his reign, the king hosted a banquet for all of his officials, including all the noble men in his provinces, so that he could display all his wealth, glory, and power. We are told that after the main celebration, which lasted for six months, another special seven-day banquet was hosted for all the palace officials and servants - from the greatest to the lowliest - and for which the courtyard was splendidly decorated.

In verse 9 we learn that at the same time as King Xerxes was hosting his banquet, Queen Vashti, the king's wife, was hosting another banquet for the women of the royal palace (Esther 1:9).

Verse 10 says that on the seventh day of the royal banquet, when the king was half drunk, he called all seven of the Eunuchs who attended him to bring him Queen Vashti, his wife, so that she could display her beauty for all the guests to see. But the queen refused to come and the king was furious. After consultation with his officials, the matter was concluded: a decision was made that, as a deterrent to all women in the land, the queen must be barred from appearing before the king ever again. This led to the deposition of Queen Vashti and led to the subsequent search for a new queen.

I am happy to remind you that Queen Vashti's refusal to appear before her husband and his guests was God's doing, because then He could favour somebody (Esther) for a special task. As a word of encouragement, therefore, let me remind you that for you to ascend to a higher position, such as to the throne of nobility, God may be partial to you and cause someone else to quit or resign in order to make way for you. Exodus 14:4 tells of God's partiality and how He will fight for your elevation: "'Then I will harden Pharaoh's heart, so that he will pursue them; and I will gain honour over Pharaoh and over all his army, that the Egyptians may know that I *am* the LORD.' And they did so."

In Esther 2:7 we read: "And *Mordecai* had brought up Hadassah, that *is,* Esther, his uncle's daughter, for she had neither father nor mother. The young woman *was* lovely and beautiful. When her father and mother died, Mordecai took her as his own daughter."

In Esther 2:15–17 it is told that: "When the turn came for Esther (the girl Mordecai had adopted, the daughter of his uncle Abihail) to go to the king, she asked for nothing other than what Hegai, the king's eunuch who was in charge of the harem, suggested. And Esther won the *favour* of everyone who saw her. She was taken to King Xerxes in the royal residence in the tenth month, the month of Tebeth, in the seventh year of his reign. Now the king was attracted to Esther more than to any of the other women, and she won his *favour* and approval more than any of the other virgins. So he set a royal crown on her head and made her queen instead of Vashti."

From the quotation we learn that Esther, the girl Mordecai had adopted, the daughter of his uncle, Abihail, who was living in exile with her people the Jews, was chosen from among many other girls to become the queen, the wife of King Xerxes, in a foreign land, because of God's favour. The girl from nowhere was lifted to the palace, the place of dignity, because she won God's favour and the king's.

What I am saying here is that God hardened Queen Vashti's heart against her husband, the king, so that an ordinary Jewish girl could be honoured by him. Likewise, somebody will give way to your honour, may the Lord harden someone's heart to give way for your exaltation. Praise God! If you believe say Amen to that.

Like me, believe that when the LORD wants to favour you He will show you partiality, even if He has to depose or dethrone someone from a position or place, as he did for Esther. Believe me, He will do it.

Finally, in chapter 1, we read in verse 17 that the king set a ***royal crown*** on Esther's head and made her queen in place of Vashti. This means that God has given his formal approval and support for Esther to become a member of the monarch's family. The king was more attracted to Esther than to any of the other women brought before him, and she won his ***favour*** and approval more than any of the other virgins. So the king set a royal crown on her head and made her queen instead of Vashti.

Verse 18 says that, to celebrate the occasion, the king gave a great banquet, Esther's banquet, for all his nobles and officials. He proclaimed a holiday throughout the provinces and distributed gifts with royal liberality. This is what favour can bring to a person.

Verse 20 tells us that Esther had kept secret her family background and nationality, just as Mordecai had instructed. For Esther continued to follow Mordecai's instructions, just as she had done all the while that Mordecai was bringing her up.

From this, it is clear that the king did not ask and, therefore, did not even know the background and nationality of Esther before he married her and made her queen. Like many of the other people discussed in this book so far, we can testify that favour made any shortcomings in a person's background irrelevant. Esther probably never dreamt that in her own life she would become a queen, not even among her own people, the Jews, yet she became Queen of Persia, in Susa, irrespective of her background. Favour will conceal your background and conceal your identity, and then promote you to a place of honour.

Like Esther, everybody has foundations, roots, origins, or ancestors to whom they are connected. It is as a result of these foundations that many people find themselves in the situations they are in today; not because they planned life in that way, but as a result of the foundations, or the roots, from which they grew and to which they are connected. Some of these people suffer from many, many ailments and restrictions, not because of something they have done wrong, but because of something which was instituted within their family, by their ancestors. On the reverse side of the coin there are also, of course, those who are benefiting from the good foundations that their ancestors or parents put down, because not all foundations, roots, or origins are bad, there are good ones too. Esther's foundations and nationality, however, were that of a Jewish girl, living with her people who were captives in Susa, under the kingship of King Xerxes. For more about people's foundations, read my book *The Power for Your Zero Hour*.

Thank God for Jesus, Whose atoning death has covered us for every sin made by man, and made us all (believers) a royal priesthood and a holy nation.

Another point I find interesting is that Esther continued to follow Mordecai's instructions, just as she had always done while he was bringing her up. This also means that Esther continued to live according to the training she had been given by Mordecai; and, as a Jew, therefore, even though she was living among heathens, she lived according the precepts of the true God of the Jews.

Unlike Esther, many people, even after God has elevated them to a higher position or place, find that out of pride they abandon the God who has elevated them. In simple terms I would suggest that some people who have benefitted from God's favour even stop going to church, while others, even though they may still attend church, become less committed to the LORD. The worst thing of all is when others hide their background or nationality. If you want to keep God's favour in your life, never abandon your God, and never hide facts about from where the LORD lifted you. Moses told the Israelites that, when they got to the Promised Land, they should never forget that it was God who gave them the power to gain wealth (Deuteronomy 8:18). Not until you acknowledge what the LORD has done for you can you truly praise Him.

In Esther 3 we learn that the favour accorded to Esther attracted the negative and dangerous attentions of Haman. Haman was honoured by the king when he decided to eliminate all the Jews from the land, by killing them, after Mordecai failed to bow before him (Haman) as he passed.

We learn of this incident in Esther 3:1–2, which reads: "After these events, King Xerxes honoured Haman son of Hammedatha, the Agagite, elevating him, and giving him a seat of honour higher than that of all the other nobles. All the royal officials at the king's gate knelt down and paid honour to Haman, for the king had commanded this concerning him. But Mordecai would not kneel down or pay him honour."

Reading further, up to verse 11, we learn how the evil Haman looked for a way to carry out his ghastly plan to kill all the Jews in King Xerxes' province. First, Haman and his supporters selected a day and month; they chose the twelfth month, the month of Adar. Secondly, in verse 8, in order to win the king's support, Haman lied about the Jews, telling the king: "There is a certain people dispersed and scattered among the peoples in all the provinces of your kingdom whose customs are different from those of all other people and who do not obey the king's laws; it is not in the king's best interest to tolerate them." With this, King Xerxes grants Haman permission to carry out his evil desire. Thirdly, to show his support, the king refused to accept the money Haman had promised to pay into the royal treasury, which Haman had pledged to pay for the men who carried out this terrible, murderous business.

In Esther 4 we read that the news that the edict had been passed by the king, erupted in great mourning among the Jews: "When Mordecai learned all that had happened, he tore his clothes and put on sackcloth and ashes, and went out into the midst of the city. He cried out with a loud and bitter cry. He went as far as the front of the king's gate, for no one *might* enter the king's gate clothed with sackcloth. And in every province where the king's command and decree arrived, *there was* great mourning among the Jews, with fasting, weeping, and wailing; and many lay in sackcloth and ashes." (Esther 4:1–3)

Queen Esther wanted to know what was happening to her people the Jews, and in her distress she sent a messenger to ask her uncle why the Jews were in mourning. Mordecai sent the messenger back to Esther to tell her everything about the edict, even sending her a copy of the document, along with a request for Esther to seek favour with her husband, the king, to intervene.

In Esther 3:13–17 we read: "And Mordecai told them to answer Esther: 'Do not think in your heart that you will escape in the king's palace any more than all the other Jews. For if you remain completely silent at this time, relief and deliverance will arise for the Jews from another place, but you and your father's house will perish. Yet who knows whether you have come to the kingdom for such a time as this?' Then Esther told them to reply to Mordecai: 'Go, gather all the Jews who are present in Shushan, and fast for me; neither eat nor drink for three days, night or day. My maids and I will fast likewise. And so I will go to the king, which is against the law; and if I perish, I perish!' So Mordecai went his way and did according to all that Esther commanded him."

Esther, who initially refused to appeal to the king, her husband, because it was against the law to appear before the king in such manner, later agreed to take the risk for the sake of her people. She sent the messenger back to Mordecai saying: "Go, gather all the Jews who are present in Shushan, and fast for me; neither eat nor drink for three days, night or day. My maids and I will fast likewise. And so I will go to the king, which *is* against the law; and if I perish, I perish!"

Looking back at Esther 3:14, remember what Mordecai told Esther: "For if you remain completely silent at this time, relief and deliverance will arise for the Jews from another place, but you and your father's house will perish. Yet who knows whether you have come to the kingdom for *such* a time as this?"

There are two points that should be highlighted here:

First: Mordecai proved his faith and confidence in God by trusting that, as a Jew, and for that matter the favoured one, God would deliver his people. I want to ask you, therefore: how far do you as a believer have faith and confidence in God? In the face of trouble are you able to believe in Him and declare your faith? Are you able to say that even if man's help fails you, you know that God will remain faithful to you?

Second: Mordecai says to Esther: "who knows whether you have come to the kingdom for *such* a time as this?" What Mordecai means by this is who knows why your favour has elevated you to the palace and made you queen, but maybe it is because of this very time, in order that you can intervene for the lives of your people. I find this a very interesting point in the context of the modern day when I hear about and witness many people abandoning their responsibilities.

First of all, every believer was saved in order to lead others to Christ, but how many believers are living up to this responsibility when so many souls are still left in the wilderness to go to hell? Jesus said that if believers respond to the Great Commission (Matthew 20:28) God will answer our prayer. He said: "You did not choose me, but I chose you and appointed you so that you might go and bear fruit—fruit that will last—and so that whatever you ask in my name the Father will give you." (John 15:16)

Secondly, many people fail to live responsibly even when they, by the favour of God, have been put in higher positions and places than others, for the blessing of others. God may elevate these people in order to become the bread winner within a family or even a community. In Genesis 12:2 the Bible says that when the LORD called Abraham He said: "I will make you into a great nation, and I will bless you; I will make your name great, and you will be a blessing."

Many people are favoured to become the wife or the husband of somebody for a reason. The LORD may make you a manager or even a Pastor, and so what are you going to do with this position? I would like to say this: if the LORD has blessed you and you are not giving blessing to others, let this message of Mordecai's to Esther speak to you, before the LORD strips you of everything.

In Esther 5 we learn how the risk Esther took was rewarded. Appearing before the king prior to the official time she was required to present herself, the king demanded to know what she wanted, he even promised to grant her whatever she asked for, even half of his kingdom. Esther's reply is written in verses 7–8: "Then Esther answered and said, 'My petition and request *is this:* if I have found favour in the sight of the king, and if it pleases the king to grant my petition and fulfil my request, then let the king and Haman come to the banquet which I will prepare for them, and tomorrow I will do as the king has said.'"

Without knowing that the favour of God was at work, in verses 9–14 we learn how Haman returned and was at first very angry, because at the gate he saw Mordecai, who still did not bow to him even after the passing of the edict. We then learn that Haman was very happy when he was told that he was invited to a banquet with the king; he went home to brag to his wife and friends, all of whom suggested that he should build a gallows from which to hang Mordecai, but unfortunately, as it turns out, Haman built his own gallows.

In Esther 7:1–4 we read that the king had trouble sleeping, so he ordered that the records of his kingdom be brought to him so that he could read them. There, he discovered what Mordecai had saved him from an attempted assassination in the past. The next day, just as he was asking his attendant's advice about how to reward Mordecai for saving his life, Haman arrived at the very same time. He had come to request the king's permission to hang Mordecai at the gallows he had just had erected.

Without knowing that the king was talking about Mordecai because of the way the question was put to him, Haman thought to himself that there is no person in the land who deserves honour more than he himself, so he said: "For the man whom the king delights to honour, let a royal robe be brought which the king has worn, and a horse on which the king has ridden, which has a royal crest placed on its head. Then let this robe and horse be delivered to the hand of one of the king's most noble princes that he may array the man whom the king delights to honour. Then parade him on horseback through the city square, and proclaim before him: 'Thus shall it be done to the man whom the king delights to honour!' Then the king said to Haman, 'Hurry, take the robe and the horse, as you have suggested, and do so for Mordecai the Jew who sits within the king's gate! Leave nothing undone of all that you have spoken.'

So Haman took the robe and the horse, arrayed Mordecai and led him on horseback through the city square, and proclaimed before him, 'Thus shall it be done to the man whom the king delights to honour!'" (Esther 6:7–11)

Verses 12–14 (NLT) continue with the story: "Afterward Mordecai returned to the palace gate, but Haman hurried home dejected and completely humiliated. When Haman told his wife, Zeresh, and all his friends what had happened, they said, 'Since Mordecai—this man who has humiliated you—is a Jew, you will never succeed in your plans against him. It will be fatal to continue to oppose him.' While they were still talking, the king's eunuchs arrived to take Haman to the banquet Esther had prepared."

I really enjoy reading about what happens when Haman arrives home in disgrace and explains to his wife, Zeresh, and all his friends the recent events: "Since Mordecai—this man who has humiliated you—is a Jew, you will never succeed in your plans against him." They are aware that Jews are favoured by God and realise that Esther is also. Thus remember: when you are favoured no one can take away anything from your life because, like the Jews, you are protected.

I recommend that you read Esther 7, where Esther reveals to the king Haman's plans to kill all the Jews, which will include herself of course, and even tells her husband, the king, how Haman had offered a reward of money to anyone who killed a Jew. Your guess is as good as mine as to what the king's reaction would be towards someone who desired to destroy his favoured wife and her people. Verse 7a reads "Then the king arose in his wrath from the banquet of wine *and went into the palace garden.*"

From verse 7b we learn that, while the king was in the garden, Haman went to Esther's table to beg for his life. Now the tables are turned: the one who previously had the power to kill is now begging for his life; Haman knew from the king's reaction that his life was at risk, but now unfortunately his actions plunged him into even more trouble. When the king returned from the garden, the king said to Haman, "Will he also assault the queen while I *am* in the house?" As the words left the king's mouth, they covered Haman's face. Reading further to the end of Esther 7, we learn that Haman was hanged at the gallows, the very gallows he himself had erected for Mordecai.

In Esther 8, we read that after the death of Haman, Esther is given his estate, and that once again she appears before the king to ask if he will reverse what has been decreed against the Jews by Haman. Interestingly, with the king's permission, Haman's evil decree is reversed and a new decree, written by the king's secretaries as dictated by Mordecai, carries the king's name and is sealed by his signet ring as if it had been written by him.

In Esther 11 we read: "By these letters the king permitted the Jews who *were* in every city to gather together and protect their lives—to destroy, kill, and annihilate all the forces of any people or province that would assault them, *both* little children and women, and to plunder their possessions."

Esther 9 records how many people the Jews killed as their enemies, including the ten sons of Haman whose evil plot backfired as a result of the decree that came into effect on the twelfth month; that *is*, the month of Adar (7 March according to the Gregorian calendar we use today), the month that is also mentioned in Esther 2:16. This, the festival of Purim, has been celebrated by the Jews every year ever since, as Mordecai decreed, saying that the time when the Jews gained relief from their enemies, when their sorrow was turned into gladness and their mourning into joy, should be commemorated.

At this point I would like to say that when you are taken to the palace, when you are promoted and lifted up in life, you may attract jealousy and hatred, both of which could threaten your life, but favour will backfire on every plot your enemies hatch against you as you are the favoured one. If the enemy plots your dismissal you will celebrate his dismissal; whatever calamity your enemy has planned against you will reflect back on him.

The four Hebrew men who received favour from King Nebuchadnezzar

These men were given new names. "To Daniel was given the name Belteshazzar; to Hananiah, Shadrach; to Mishael, Meshach; and to Azariah, Abednego. The king assigned them a daily amount of food and wine from the king's table. They were to be trained for three years, and after that they were to enter the king's service." (Daniel 1:7)

Favour gives you access, but as further reading shows, Daniel resisted the opportunity for himself and his compatriots to eat at the king's table. Instead, Daniel requested that something different be given to them because he believed that the royal food and wine on offer could defile them. Personally, I see favour at another level here. The guests were selected to dine at the king's table, but requested special food because they were foreigners. To me, this means that they were able to take advantage of their status as foreigners by refusing the king's food, and requesting food that they believed was better for them.

In Daniel 1:9–10 it is clear that even though the king's official in charge of Daniel knew that his life would be in danger if he did anything against the king's order, that is, to offer the Jews something different to eat and drink, yet God caused the official to show favour and sympathy towards Daniel's request. As I assured you earlier, when you are favoured, people will be willing to do things for you, even if doing so may put at risk his own life or job, just as the official granted Daniel's request.

Interestingly, in Daniel 1:13–16 we read: "Then compare our appearance with that of the young men who eat the royal food, and treat your servants in accordance with what you see. So he agreed to this and tested them for ten days. At the end of the ten days they looked healthier and better nourished than any of the young men who ate the royal food. So the guard took away their choice food and the wine they were to drink and gave them vegetables instead."

The attitude of Daniel and his companions is a lesson to us all: we don't always have to bow to the demands of our bosses or anybody else above us, especially when their demands could have a bad effect on our Christian life or our relationship with God. With our prayers and our faith in God, our superiors will heed what we tell them in the end. Personally, I feel that it is very sad when people succumb to requests for the sake of money or position, even though this may damage their relationship with God.

Similar to Daniel and his three companions, David refused to wear Saul's armour saying, "I have not proved this"; in other words he is saying that I have never used this type of weapon before (1 Samuel 17:38–40).

Again, let me say, it is sad that one can point to the many times when some Christians have failed to declare their stand and faith in God in the midst of confrontation. In the midst of confrontation and difficult situations, many believers fail even to declare that they are Christians. This is especially difficult to understand, and one wonders why they do not appreciate that their brothers are around. Have these people forgotten that our Omnipresent God is always there watching and ready to support us?

Again, it was Daniel who found favour in the eyes of King Darius, who then lifted him to a high position: "It pleased Darius to appoint 120 satraps to rule throughout the kingdom, with three administrators over them, one of whom was Daniel. The satraps were made accountable to them so that the king might not suffer loss. Now Daniel so distinguished himself among the administrators and the satraps by his exceptional qualities that the king planned to set him over the whole kingdom." (Daniel 6:1–3)

But as is often the case with favour, Daniel's favour attracted the jealousy and hatred of the other administrators, which brought him trouble. The other administrators tried to find grounds for charges against Daniel in his conduct of government affairs, but they were unable to find grounds for such an accusation. They could find no corruption in him, because he was trustworthy and neither corrupt nor negligent.

After trying everything they could, but find nothing, they had to admit defeat: "We will never find any basis for charges against this man Daniel unless it has something to do with the law of his God."

Having tried to find something against him, Daniel's enemies then succeeded in getting the king's consent to a law. This law meant that whoever petitioned any god or man for thirty days, except the king, shall be cast into the lions' den.

Daniel 6:10 reads: "Now when Daniel learned that the decree had been published, he went home to his upstairs room where the windows opened toward Jerusalem. Three times a day he got down on his knees and prayed, giving thanks to his God, just as he had done before."

As a result, Daniel was put into the lions' den, but even in the lions' den God's favour followed him, so that he avoided coming to any harm from the lions.

Finally Daniel 6:18–22 says: "Then the king returned to his palace and spent the night without eating and without any entertainment being brought to him. And he could not sleep. At the first light of dawn, the king got up and hurried to the lions' den. When he came near the den, he called to Daniel in an anguished voice, 'Daniel, servant of the living God, has your God, whom you serve continually, been able to rescue you from the lions?' Daniel answered, 'O king, live forever! My God sent his angel and he shut the mouths of the lions. They have not hurt me, because I was found innocent in his sight. Nor have I ever done any wrong before you, O king.'"

I believe that at this time it was against the king's own law for him to visit Daniel at the lions' den; yet the king risked his position because of his love for Daniel; and the king's love for Daniel was due to God's favour.

Prayer pattern: Declare the favour of God through prayers

1. That will cause somebody to remember you or your case;
2. That will cause someone not to rest until s/he has fulfilled what is due to you:
   + Daniel 6:18: "then the king returned to his palace and spent the night without eating and without any entertainment being brought to him. And he could not sleep."
3. That will cause someone to dream about you:
   + Matthew 27:19: "while Pilate was sitting on the judge's seat, his wife sent him this message: 'Don't have anything to do with that innocent man, for I have suffered a great deal today in a dream because of him.'"

4. That will cause someone to come to your aid or rescue you from your difficulty, such as a lack of money. Not only believers benefit, but unbelievers benefit as well. After all, the Bible says that "the wealth of the unrighteous is stored for the righteous." (Proverbs 13:32)

THE ASSURANCE OF FAVOUR

Who are the favoured?

Maybe after hours or days of reading this book, or having been hearing me preach, you may be wondering who are the favoured and who is entitled to the LORD's favour and all of its benefits. I would like now to let you know who are the favoured.

In my recent book *Be Ye Transformed* I dealt with salvation and also treated assurance of salvation. This is because I know that there are many Christians who are still not sure whether they are really saved or not. I cited as an example the response of a woman after I had asked her if she was sure that she was destined for heaven when she died. She replied to me very angrily saying, "How should I know if I will go to heaven when I die, it is only God who knows."

In *Be Ye Transformed* I argued that, "Being certain of your salvation is as important as being born again. When you are not sure of what you have, you can easily loose it, so it is better to be certain in the knowledge that you are saved." I also mentioned that there are certain people, maybe because they are not sure of their salvation, and in their ignorance, who at every meeting or crusade respond to altar call; and I mentioned others who use altar call to go forward in order that they will be prayed for on other issues.

The three quotations below all support my assurance of our salvation, but there are many, many more, these are just a selection.

John 1:11–13

"He came to that which was his own, but his own did not receive him. Yet to all who received him, to those who believed in his name, he gave the right to become children of God—children born not of natural descent, nor of human decision or a husband's will, but born of God."

Galatians 3:26–29

"You are all sons of God through faith in Christ Jesus, for all of you who were baptised into Christ have clothed yourselves with Christ. There is neither Jew nor Greek, slave nor free, male nor female, for you are all one in Christ Jesus. If you belong to Christ, then you are Abraham's seed, and heirs according to the promise."

1 John 5:1

"Everyone who believes that Jesus is the Christ is born of God, and everyone who loves the father loves his child as well."

There are so many more quotations in the Bible that help one to be sure of one's salvation, which is to say that when one comes to being fully convinced that one is saved by Christ, one is helped to live for Christ and also to submit to His will.

I consider **assurance of favour** as equal in importance to assurance of salvation. But what do I mean by assurance of favour? I believe, without any doubt, that after many days or hours of reading or hearing about favour and all that goes with it, still someone may struggle to grasp this life-changing message, and will continue to find it difficult to pray for or declare the favour of God upon him or herself.

What I mean by **assurance of favour** is summed up in the few statements below:

- ✦ I want you to be sure you are favoured;
- ✦ I want you to be able to say "I am favoured";
- ✦ I want you to know that you are entitled to the favour of God as a believer;
- ✦ I want you to know that God has already declared that you are favoured; He did this on the very day that you received Christ as LORD and personal saviour, so that you can declare it, just as you feel free to declare or say that you are saved.

Key quotation: Psalms 5:11–12

"But let all who take refuge in you be glad; let them ever sing for joy. Spread your protection over them, that is, those who love your name may rejoice in you. For surely, O LORD, you bless the righteous; you surround them with your favour as with a shield." (NIV)

"But let all those rejoice who put their trust in You; let them ever shout for joy, because You defend them; let those also who love Your name Be joyful in You. For You, O LORD, will bless the righteous; with favour You will surround him as with a shield." (NKJV)

Our assurance/your assurance/my assurance

Psalms 5:12 says that God has surrounded the righteous with favour, like a shield.

The Amplify Bible Verse 12 says:

"For you, LORD, will bless the [uncompromisingly] righteous [he who is upright and in right standing with you]: as with shield You will surround him with goodwill [pleasure and favour]."

Before we are able to grasp the truth of this Psalm, we should seek to understand what a shield is and then explore who are the righteous:

1. A shield is a flat or convex piece of armour carried on the arm and used as protection against blows (from weapons), arrows, bullets, or projectiles. To shield can also be used as a verb, meaning to protect, to safeguard, to defend, and to arm.

2. Righteousness, on the other hand, is considered correct or justifiable. In other words, it is one who is justified, just, or right in what they do. In the Bible, righteousness is used in three different ways:

    1. It describes what God is like, which means that He does only what is right and holy.

2. It is used to describe those who have accepted Jesus as LORD and Saviour, because they are considered by God as being free from the guilt of sin.

3. When believers show their love for God by living righteously, that is, when they do what is right and holy, then the righteousness of God is manifest in their lives.

Now, in order to look to the question concerning who is the favoured and to try to answer it, I would like to draw from point 2 above, which suggests that all believers are righteous and therefore favoured, or surrounded by favour, in the context of Psalm 5:12. Believers are the justified and, therefore, the righteous, because we have faith in Christ.

To prove the point I have made above, I have selected a few quotations from the Bible (below), of which there are many, many more, to prove that our faith in Christ makes us righteous.

2 Corinthians 5:21

"For He made Him who knew no sin to be sin for **us**, that we might become the righteousness of God in Him."

To intersect my commentary with quotations from the Bible, in order to contemplate the notion that we are all favoured, is what this book is about. Below are some further quotations.

Isaiah 53:6

Describing the coming Messiah, Isaiah says: "We all, like sheep, have gone astray, each of us has turned to his own way; and the LORD has laid on him the iniquity of *us* all."

Isaiah 53:9

"He was assigned a grave with the wicked and with the rich in his death, though he had done no violence, nor was any deceit in his mouth."

Jeremiah 23:6

Jeremiah describes Him as the LORD our righteous (Jehovah Tsidekenu). "In his days Judah will be saved and Israel will live in safety. This is the name by which he will be called: The LORD Our Righteousness."

Galatians 3:13–14

"Christ redeemed *us* from the curse of the law by becoming a curse for *us,* for it is written: 'Cursed is everyone who is hung on a tree.' He redeemed us in order that the blessing given to Abraham might come to the Gentiles through Christ Jesus, so that by faith we might receive the promise of the Spirit.'"

1 Peter 2:22–24

Describing his master, Peter told his readers: "He committed no sin, and no deceit was found in his mouth. When they hurled their insults at him, he did not retaliate; when he suffered, he made no threats. Instead, he entrusted himself to him who judges justly. He himself bore *our* sins in his body on the tree, so that we might die to sin and live for righteousness; by his wounds you have been healed."

Are you seeing a picture here? What I see appearing is the image that through Christ, we (believers) became sons of God in the same way that, through Him, God has made us righteous. So I would like you to know that you and I, as believers, are surrounded by, or protected, by God's favour.

The need for this assurance

Just as not all believers are sure of their salvation, in the same way, many believers may not be sure of God's favour in their lives.

Some might say: It is Noah, the Israelites, Moses, Abraham, Jacob, Joseph, David, Samuel, Esther, Daniel and the three Hebrew men, and many more as we have heard, that deserve God's favour, not me. **No, that is ignorance!** The truth of the matter is that every believer is a child of God. We are all entitled to His divine favour, and that is why I declare to you that you are favoured by God and therefore entitled to all the benefits of His favour.

Prayer pattern

I believe that, having been able to bring you to the knowledge that you are favoured, because of the work of Jesus on the cross, you will now be able to declare without any doubt in your mind that you are favoured.

Many times we sing "I am a winner, the favour of God is upon me, and the devil knows that I am a winner." Yes, the devil knows that you are a winner, but my question and my concern is this: do you actually believe that for yourself? Again, Arch Bishop Benson Idahosa once said: "the Devil knows who we are as children of God, but what is not sure is whether we believers know who we are in God, that is why he always tempts us to see if we know who we are. If you know, then begin to declare your favour now."

Primarily, as you declare the favour of God over your life, I want you to understand that God's favour is activated, just as it already has been in your life. Favour in a believer's life is like the tap you turn on for water or the gas-pipe fittings, both of which bring these utilities into our homes. That is to say, like God's favour, they are already there, but you have to turn them on. You might see God's favour as a bank debit or credit card, which needs activating before you can use it.

Secondly, in declaring the LORD's favour, in the spiritual realm, you are declaring:

- ✦ Even though I may not have been too long in this or that country and thus may not be qualified, I am a member of the righteous family and so I do qualify. (John 1:12)
- ✦ I am qualified because I have a promise from God that wherever my foot touches, the LORD has given it to me.
- ✦ As a member of the righteous family, even though I came last, I will be above only, for as a child of God I am the head not the tail.
- ✦ As a member of the righteous family I know no defeat; I am victorious.

✦ As a member of the righteous family, even though I may not be the most beautiful or the most educated person on the list, yet I will be picked. David was chosen and anointed as the King of Israel, even though he was the youngest and his father rejected him, sending him to look after the sheep. I once heard the testimony of a man who was going to an interview, but when he arrived at the venue and realised that many people had higher certificates than his own he was tempted to abandon the interview. However, he listened to his Spirit, which told him to wait, so he waited, and then entered the room for the interview. A few days after the interview, he received a call to say that he had been awarded the job; yes, ahead of all those who had higher certificates than his own. Isn't this evidence of God's favour? Surely it must be.

In declaring the favour of God you are saying:

✦ Because Christ has qualified me to be a member of God's family, no form of weapon against me will prosper.

✦ As a member of the righteous family, yes, I may have made a lot of mistakes in the past, but that is past, and I am now a new man. The old things have passed away; behold everything has become new!

✦ You are assigning someone—not a lesser person, but a superior person in fact, to show you kindness or to go somewhere on your behalf to do something for you.

✦ You are declaring, "I will be shown partiality wherever I go."

What you are saying is: "I am protected, my life is secured": As Solomon said (Proverbs 16:7, ANIV), "When a man's ways are pleasing to the Lord, he makes even his enemies live at peace with him." In other words, when a man is favoured by God he makes even his enemies live at peace with him.

When you are favoured you are protected

Noah and his family were saved from the Flood because Noah was found to be righteous, but everybody and everything else was destroyed by God: "So the Lord said, 'I will wipe mankind, whom I have created, from the face of the earth—men and animals, and creatures that move along the ground, and birds of the air—for I am grieved that I have made them.' But Noah found favour in the eyes of the Lord." (Genesis 6:7–8)

As result of Noah's favour from the LORD, God reveals his plans to him:

"This is the account of Noah. Noah was a righteous man, blameless among the people of his time, and he walked with God. Noah had three sons: Shem, Ham and Japheth. Now the earth was corrupt in God's sight and was full of violence. God saw how corrupt the earth had become, for all the people on earth had corrupted their ways. So God said to Noah, 'I am going to put an end to all people, for the earth is filled with violence because of them. I am surely going to destroy both them and the earth. So make yourself an ark of cypress wood; make rooms in it and coat it with pitch inside and out.'" (Genesis 6:9–14, NIV)

While Genesis 6:15-16 describes how the ark must be built, Gen 6:17–22 provides details of God's plan:

"'I am going to bring floodwaters on the earth to destroy all life under the heavens, every creature that has the breath of life in it. Everything on earth will perish. But I will establish my covenant with you, and you will enter the ark—you and your sons and your wife and your sons' wives with you. You are to bring into the ark two of all living creatures, male and female, to keep them alive with you. Two of every kind of bird, of every kind of animal and of every kind of creature that moves along the ground will come to you to be kept alive. You are to take every kind of food that is to be eaten and store it away as food for you and for them.' Noah did everything just as God commanded him."

Noah obeys God and builds the ark:

"The LORD then said to Noah, 'Go into the ark, you and your whole family, because I have found you righteous in this generation. Take with you seven of every kind of clean animal, a male, and its mate, and two of every kind of unclean animal, a male and its mate, and also seven of every kind of bird, male and female, to keep their various kinds alive throughout the earth. Seven days from now I will send rain on the earth for forty days and forty nights, and I will wipe from the face of the earth every living creature I have made.' And Noah did all that the LORD commanded him." (Genesis 7:1–5)

"Noah was six hundred years old when the floodwaters came on the earth. And Noah and his sons and his wife and his sons' wives entered the ark to escape the waters of the flood." (Genesis 7:6–7)

Then, as Genesis 7:16–24 describes:

"After Noah and his family entered the ark with all the animals as the Lord had commanded him **the Lord shut the door**. The rain came down and the waters flooded the earth for a hundred and fifty days until every living creature was destroyed except Noah and all those who were with him in the ark."

Praise God! Noah found God's favour because he was a righteous man. And, as a result, Noah and his family were saved from the wrath of God.

After entering the ark, the Bible says that **"the Lord shut the door"**, making it most secure, and watertight. When God shuts a door no one or anything can open it, and because Christ has made us all open to the righteousness of God, so God has surrounded us with His favour. Thus it is that we are all secure, and believers are protected.

FAVOUR BRINGS CONFIDENCE

The writer of the book of Hebrews said: "Let us then approach God's throne of grace with confidence, so that we may receive mercy and find grace to help us in our time of need." (Hebrews 4:16)

When you know that you have found favour in God's sight or in the sight of men, you will have confidence to demand anything you want without any fear. A child will have the confidence to ask his or her parents for anything they want when they realise that they have found favour in the sight of their parents, and especially when they know they have done something that pleases their parents. For example, my daughter always asks me to take her to McDonald's or buy her a pizza when she knows that she has won my approval maybe because of her achievements at school or something special she has done.

✦ Moses' confidence to ask God for what he wants

"Moses said to the LORD, 'You have been telling me, "Lead these people," but you have not let me know whom you will send with me. You have said, "I know you by name and you have found favour with me." If you are pleased with me, teach me your ways so I may know you and continue to find favour with you. Remember that this nation is your people.' The LORD replied, 'My Presence will go with you, and I will give you rest.' Then Moses said to him, 'If your Presence does not go with us, do not send us up from here. How will anyone know that you are pleased with me and with your people unless you go with us? What else will distinguish me and your people from all the other people on the face of the earth?' And the LORD said to Moses, 'I will do the very thing you have asked, because I am pleased with you and I know you by name.'" (Exodus 33:12–17)

To gain more understanding, may I suggest that you read the background of the story from verse 1.

From verse 12, above, we understand that Moses said to the LORD, "If you are pleased with me", in other words Moses is saying: if I have found favour in your sight teach me your ways so that I may know you and continue to find favour with you. Moses' statement, in short, means that when you know the ways of God you will also find the favour of the LORD.

Divine favour brings the presence of God into this context also: "The LORD replied, 'My Presence will go with you, and I will give you rest.'" Also, when Moses knew he had found favour in God he demanded that God himself went with them, not an angel, and the LORD heeded his request. This indicates that favour also brings access: when you know you are favoured, you have access to the presence of God and to man.

In Exodus 33:2, the LORD promised to send his angel to go before the Israelites, but Moses refused the offer saying, in verses 15 and 16: "If your Presence does not go with us, do not send us up from here. How will anyone know that you are pleased with me and with your people unless you go with us? What else will distinguish me and your people from all the other people on the face of the earth?"

When you are favoured, you are distinguishable among others and become different.

I wonder why Moses refused to go with an angel, since we know from the scriptures that God uses angels to deliver His people from trouble or to deliver messages. One such incidence is that recorded by the Prophet Isaiah: "Then the angel of the LORD went out and put to death a hundred and eighty-five thousand men in the Assyrian camp. When the people got up the next morning—there were all the dead bodies! So Sennacherib King of Assyria broke camp and withdrew. He returned to Nineveh and stayed there." (Isaiah 37:36–37)

I would like to believe that Moses was saying, no matter what an angel could do for us, at this point, we need you, for your presence supersedes any effort by any of your angels.

Another point of interest for me is how Moses could be so bold as to refuse God's offer; how did he have the courage to turn down God's proposal for them to go with an angel? My view of this is that when you are favoured, you have access to God's heart without fear; His favour will grant you boldness. When one knows that special kindness is being shown to one by someone superior, one will take advantage of that favour.

Like Moses, all believers through Christ are favoured, as we learnt earlier, and therefore all believers have access to the throne of grace. This is as the writer of Hebrews (4:16) tells us.

And this is why it is very important to be sure that you are favoured; for unless you know you are favoured you cannot take advantage of favour.

In my conclusion to this section, let me offer these words:

Moses demonstrates his boldness by refusing God's offer of sending an angel to go with him and the Israelites, because he had found favour in the sight of God; so the LORD changed his mind and said "I will go with you and give you rest." This means that, with the favour of God, you will be delivered from any calamity, you and your family will be securely protected, and there can be no intruders in your life. When you are favoured, in the context of Exodus 33:12–17, and as a member of the righteous family, you have access into God's heart, the throne of grace, and so you have a choice to tell even God Himself what you want. What a privilege!

I would like to remind you of Esther's story as I conclude this section of the book, "Favour brings confidence". Esther, knowing that she has favour from the king, took advantage and asked for more of whatever she wanted, even asking for more powers for the Jews to kill all the enemies of the Israelites.

In chapter 5:8 she says: "If I have found favour in the sight of the king, and if it pleases the king to grant my petition and fulfil my request, then let the king and Haman come to the banquet which I will prepare for them, and tomorrow I will do as the king has said."

Also in chapter 7:3 we learn: "Then Queen Esther answered and said, 'If I have found favour in your sight, O king, and if it pleases the king, let my life be given me at my petition, and my people at my request.'"

And in chapter 8:5-6 Esther says, "If it pleases the king, and if I have found favour in his sight and the thing *seems* right to the king and I am pleasing in his eyes, let it be written to revoke the letters devised by Haman, the son of Hammedatha the Agagite, which he wrote to annihilate the Jews who *are* in all the king's provinces. For how can I endure to see the evil that will come to my people? Or how can I endure to see the destruction of my countrymen?" And in 9:1-21 Esther asks for powers to kill the enemies of the Jews.

Why don't you take advantage of the favour of God, which comes through Jesus, in your life?

FAVOUR CAN BE BOTH ACQUIRED AND EARNED

From the previous section we have learnt that favour is an act of God. If somebody does something for somebody else under the influence of God; if somebody does something for somebody else knowing that the person does not really deserve it, or has never done anything that makes him or her deserving of the favour, this is an act of God. Yet, I would also like to show you another aspect of favour that I have come to know and which I believe many do not know.

What I have come to know is this: favour can be acquired or earned as well. So is there a contradiction here? Not at all, for as noted earlier, the sovereignty of God can be applied here too. He is an unquestionable God whose work is always right. There are four ways I have come to know, through study, that favour can be acquired or earned in the same way as God himself bestows favour to a person from His own will and for His own purpose. The four ways are:

- ✦ Through sacrifice or giving;
- ✦ Through prayer;
- ✦ Through love and faithfulness;
- ✦ Through faith in God.

God will grant you favour through your sacrifice or giving; in Genesis 4:4–5 we read: "But Abel brought fat portions from some of the firstborn of his flock. The Lord looked with favour on Abel and his offering, but on Cain and his offering he did not look with favour. So Cain was very angry, and his face was downcast."

The scripture quoted above says that while the Lord looked at Abel's sacrifice with favour, he did not look at Cain's with favour. In the context of this part of the book, I want you to consider why Abel had earned favour from the Lord, but Cain had not. Why might that be? I'll tell you why, because Abel brought fat portions from some of the firstborn of his flock, which means he brought to the Lord the best of his flock for the sacrifice.

Giving the best to the LORD will earn you His favour, which will open doors for you to be favoured by others, just as Luke said: "Give, and it will be given to you: good measure, pressed down, shaken together, and running over will be put into your bosom. For with the same measure that you use, it will be measured back to you." (Luke 6:38)

People will bestow on you or render any services unto you when you have done nothing to deserve it, but only when you have won favour in their sight. Give to God, and give to Him willingly the best that you have, and you will be favoured.

It is for this reason that in Genesis (32:13, 20) Jacob tried to give gifts to his brother Esau. This was in order to win his brother's favour, since his brother, whom he had not seen for almost twenty years, had wanted to kill him after Jacob deceived their father Isaac for the blessing that was meant for Esau (Genesis 27:41).

1 Samuel 25, especially verses 27–35, relates specifically to the subject of this part of the book. My advice to you is to read this interesting story. With her gifts of food and her wise words, Abigail won the favour of David. In turn, David spared the life of Abigail's husband and all the males of their household.

The LORD appears to Solomon when he sacrificed to the LORD for the favour shown to him

Solomon, a man whose life reads as a roller-coaster, appears again here. In the Book of Kings we learn that he was favoured to succeed his father as King of Israel even though the background of his parents' marriage could have disqualified him. Secondly, we see what happens when he abused the favour; his life ends in anti-climax. In 1 Kings, chapter 3 we are taught another lesson about him.

Many are aware of Solomon asking God and God granting Solomon wisdom, we know that he became the wisest man in his day. However, I don't think many people are aware of what led to Solomon being granted such wisdom by God. 1 Kings 3:1–15 offers a very salient lesson about how Solomon honoured God by offering a sacrifice, and how this moved God to tell him to ask for anything he wanted.

In verses 4–5 we read: "The king went to Gibeon to offer sacrifices, for that was the most important high place, and Solomon offered a thousand burnt offerings on that altar. At Gibeon the LORD appeared to Solomon during the night in a dream, and God said, 'Ask for whatever you want me to give you.'" (1 Kings 3:4–5)

In verses 6–9 Solomon asks for wisdom: in verse 6, Solomon replies to the Lord, "You have shown great kindness to your servant, my father David, because he was faithful to you and righteous and upright in heart. You have continued this great kindness to him and have given him a son to sit on his throne this very day."

In this verse, Solomon acknowledges that God showed kindness or favour to his father. Solomon knows that God will continue to show kindness or favour to him, the father's son.

In verses 10–14 the Lord promises to give Solomon the wisdom he has requested and He even offers Solomon other things he didn't ask for.

From verses 16–28, God reveals the first test of Solomon's wisdom, when Solomon gave a wise ruling concerning a case of two women prostitutes who had come to him to seek judgement.

Solomon encourages giving

Solomon, knowing that giving to God and man can promote more favour, said this in Proverbs: "A gift opens the way and ushers the giver into the presence of the great." (Proverbs 18:16)

The quotation above, along with several others, suggests to me another way one can make his way to the palace, the place of dignity and of exaltation. This way is to be a giver.

Also in chapter 19:6 it is stated, "Many entreat the favour of the nobility, and every man *is* a friend to one who gives gifts" I believe that what the writer is trying to say here is this: many people would like to gain favour with noble people or superior people, but what people fail to grasp is that everyone is a friend to him who gives gifts; in other words, everyone would like to be around those who give gifts.

We all need and require favour from God, whatever social class, whether inferior or superior, the one who gives gift will have a greater chance of being offered favour, because a giver is a friend, as Solomon said. Your giving will make you a friend to God as well as to men, even to those in higher places, and you will be offered favour whenever you need it. Solomon was given more favour after he had made a great sacrifice to the LORD.

Acts, chapter 10 tells the story of Peter's encounter with Cornelius - a centurion in what was known as the Italian Regiment - and his household whose

Godliness rendered unto them the baptism of the Holy Spirit. I would like to say that even though the word favour is not mentioned, yet it is clear that God favoured Cornelius, not for his prayers alone, but also for his generous giving to those in need. In Acts 10:1-4 we read: "At Caesarea there was a man named Cornelius, a centurion in what was known as the Italian Regiment. He and all his family were devout and God-fearing; he gave generously to those in need and prayed to God regularly. One day at about three in the afternoon he had a vision. He distinctly saw an angel of God, who came to him and said, 'Cornelius!' Cornelius stared at Him in fear. 'What is it, Lord?' he asked. The angel answered, 'Your prayers and gifts to the poor have come up as a memorial offering before God.'"

I do sometimes wonder why some people, even believers who want to be blessed by God, seem to reject and do not even try to get to know about one of the things that provokes God's blessing, that is, by giving. Without doubt, there are some people, even in the house of God, who are using dubious means to collect money and other material things, which they do in order to enrich their own lives. In spite of this, I still maintain that the word of God still stands, and approves giving to God and to man, which will open doors for His blessings. Many have left their church with the contention that giving, and more precisely giving money, is too often preached there. To me, these people are running from God's favour; favour that will usher them into greatness through His blessing.

Worst of all are those who do not give anything, but will also try in all ways they can to discourage others within the church to give; they spread among the people all sorts of lies, either about the Pastor or something about the church. I remember, years ago, before I was called into the ministry, I gave a large amount of money to the church that I belonged to at the time. After the service, a relation of mine called me over and advised me very strongly never to give such a large sum of money to the church again. I was very surprised to hear this from someone whom previously I had looked up to for inspiration, because I thought she was mature in God, and also she was a member of the leadership team.

I thank God that even though I could not tell her what I really thought, I did not take her advice about not giving to the church. There are many people of this sort operating in churches today and, yet, these people are also looking to God to bless them financially. I don't think this will work out for them. Give to God, no matter what level you are at in life, for this will provoke Him to grant you favour. And then, even when you know you are favoured, like Solomon, show your appreciation to the LORD for His favour and He will bless you even more. As much as I advise you to be careful in where you direct your giving, by knowing the type of soil you are putting your seed into, I also advise you not to allow anyone to deter you from giving to God and your fellow men.

1. Through Prayer

Remember that in the Book of Nehemiah we learn how he prayed to God to grant him favour from the king, to allow him to go back and rebuild the walls and gates of Jerusalem after they had been destroyed by fire. Nehemiah prayed, "LORD, let your ear be attentive to the prayer of this your servant and to the prayer of your servants who delight in revering your name. Give your servant success today by granting him favour in the presence of this man. I was cupbearer to the king." (Nehemiah 1:11)

The LORD answered Nehemiah's prayer and granted him his request from King Artaxerxes, who sent him to Jerusalem with all the other materials he would need for his task, because he had His favour (Nehemiah 2:1–8).

Nehemiah 2:8 asks: "And may I have a letter to Asaph, keeper of the royal park, so he will give me timber to make beams for the gates of the citadel by the temple and for the city wall and for the residence I will occupy?" And then he tells us, "And because the gracious hand of my God was on me, the king granted my requests."

Nehemiah's story is a clear indication that you can pray for favour from God, just as you can pray for anything else. The LORD will answer by granting it to you, allowing you to carry out any task or receive anything from anywhere. Some people can only be approached when the favour of God is upon your life. There are some things you are able to receive in life only through the favour of God. You need only the favour of God in order to be given the position you need. By reason of favour, everything that has been broken, even raised to the ground with fire, can be restored in Jesus' name.

Another time, when I was leading a prayer meeting during which we were praying for the favour of God, the Spirit of the LORD told me that sometimes men need favour from their wives, wives need favour from their husbands, and sometimes parents need favour from their children and vice versa.

When the LORD grants a person favour in the sight of another person, such as your boss, husband, wife, parents, or child/children, they will view you with the compassion necessary to enable them to provide or respond to anything that you may need. Nehemiah was granted his heart's desire by the king, which was to return to Jerusalem, even though he was a captive in exile. This is because he prayed for favour from the LORD. Pray for God's favour today as you hear me preach or read this book; for whatever impossible task is ahead of you, the LORD, who listens and answers all the prayers of his children, will answer you as he did Nehemiah. As Jesus said, "ask and it shall be given".

2. Love and faithfulness

In Proverbs 3:3–4 Solomon said: "Let love and faithfulness never leave you; bind them around your neck, write them on the tablet of your heart. Then you will win favour and a good name in the sight of God and man". When your heart is filled with love and faithfulness, like a necklace around your neck, according to Solomon God will look to you with favour.

Ruth found favour in the sight of Boaz (Ruth 2:8–9) because of the love and kindness or faithfulness she showed to Naomi, her mother-in-law. In verses 10 and 11 we read: "Ruth fell at his feet and thanked him warmly. 'Why are you being so kind to me?' she asked, 'I am only a foreigner.' 'Yes, I know,' Boaz replied. 'But I also know about the love and kindness you have shown your mother-in-law since the death of your husband. I have heard how you left your father and mother and your own land to live here among complete strangers.'" (NLT)

When you love other people and show kindness or love to them, then you will also receive kindness or favour in return.

In Ruth 2:13, Ruth says to Boaz, "'I hope I continue to please you, sir. ... You have comforted me by speaking so kindly to me, even though I am not as worthy as your workers.'" This verse supports the point I have already made in this book, that when you know you are favoured you have the confidence and boldness necessary to ask for more. In this verse, Ruth is asking for more of God's favour; she is saying that if she has already found favour in God's sight, then may He continue to favour her. And Ruth's request was granted, because she then became the wife of Boaz.

Isn't it uplifting to know what favour can do for you? Ruth went to Boaz's field with the simple intention of finding something to eat for herself and her mother-in-law Naomi, but she ended up becoming the wife of a wealthy man and, above all, she became an ancestor of our LORD and Saviour Jesus Christ.

Here is the story of how favour shone on Ruth initially: "Now there was a wealthy and influential man in Bethlehem named Boaz, who was a relative of Naomi's husband, Elimelech. One day Ruth said to Naomi, 'Let me go out into the fields to gather leftover grain behind anyone who will let me do it.' And Naomi said, 'All right, my daughter, go ahead.' So Ruth went out to gather grain behind the harvesters. And as it happened, she found herself working in a field that belonged to Boaz, the relative of her father-in-law, Elimelech. While she was there, Boaz arrived from Bethlehem and greeted the harvesters." (Ruth 2:1–4)

Favour knows no bounds! It will take you anywhere you want to go, even above and beyond your wildest dreams. I think the best advice I can give you today, as you read this book or listen to me preach, is this: seek favour by accepting Jesus Christ as the ultimate favour into your life if you don't know Him already, or seek favour if you are already a believer, by praying to God to show you His favour today. Alternatively, or as well, do things that attract His favour, and your life will change forever. Amen.

King Solomon, in Proverbs 11:27, said:

"Whoever seeks good finds favour, but evil comes to one who searches for it."

"He who earnestly seeks good finds favour, but trouble will come to him who seeks evil."

To seek means to search for, that is to say, to try to find a person, thing, or place. So in this context, the scripture is saying that when one tries to do good unto others, that is, show kindness and a generous character in relation to another or others, you will also find favour.

   a. But trouble comes to those who seek evil, that is, when one desires evil to happen to another person, evil will befall him, for man will reap whatever he sows as the Psalmist said:

"Whoever is pregnant with evil conceives trouble and gives birth to disillusionment. Whoever digs a hole and scoops it out falls into the pit they have made. The trouble they cause recoils on them; their violence comes down on their own heads." (Psalms 7:14–16)

On the other hand, by way of conclusion to this section of the book, I can testify to you about the power and the advantage of favour. I have prayed for many people whose situations looked impossible, but after telling them that, even though their situation may look impossible, I am none the less praying for them that the LORD will grant them favour in whatever help they are seeking, all these people's situations were turned upside down and worked out in their favour.

3. Through faith

Favour can be acquired or earned through faith. Remember the story we considered under the heading "Favour brings God's provision and healing". In this story we heard how Jesus Christ (quoted in Luke 4:25–30) told the stories of the widow of Zarephath and Naaman the Syrian, this is further to his speech in the synagogue in Nazareth, as told in Luke 4:16.

I have connected these stories to faith, because the scriptures say that Jesus Christ read what the Prophet

Isaiah wrote many years before (see Isaiah 61:1–2) and the incident is also recorded in Luke 4:18–21: "'The Spirit of the LORD is on me, because he has anointed me to preach good news to the poor. He has sent me to proclaim freedom for the prisoners and recovery of sight for the blind, to release the oppressed, to proclaim the year of the LORD's favour.' Then he rolled up the scroll, gave it back to the attendant and sat down. The eyes of everyone in the synagogue were fastened on him, and he began by saying to them, 'Today this scripture is fulfilled in your hearing.'"

Further reading reveals the heart of what Jesus is saying in verse 21: "Today this scripture is fulfilled in your hearing." What this means, and was probably understood by Jesus' audience, is that Jesus is claiming that He is the prophet who is being written about. But the saddest part of the story, which also relates to faith, is that instead of the audience being happy and counting themselves lucky that the prophecy had been fulfilled in their lifetime, they all became angry and wanted to kill Jesus. As a result of this, in verse 24, Jesus said: "'Truly I tell you ... no prophet is accepted in his hometown.'"

Now, to get to the main point of the story: in Luke 4:25–30, when Jesus quotes the story of a widow in Zarephath in the region of Sidon (recorded in 1

Kings 17:7–17), and also tells the story of Naaman the Syrian (also recorded in 2 Kings 5:1–14), he says: "I assure you that there were many widows in Israel in Elijah's time, when the sky was shut for three and a half years and there was a severe famine throughout the land. Yet Elijah was not sent to any of them, but to a widow in Zarephath in the region of Sidon. And there were many in Israel with leprosy in the time of the Prophet Elisha, yet not one of them was cleansed— only Naaman the Syrian."

By telling this story, Jesus was telling the people that just as in the days of Elijah and Elisha, only these two people – the widow in Zarephath and Naaman the Syrian – were connected to God. He is saying that their faith in the prophets connected them to God and, therefore, they received a miracle from God. This is because in those days, after the death of King Solomon, kingship ceased to be medium through which God governed his people. The introduction of the prophets became the medium through which God governed his people, and the Age of the Prophets had begun.

Well you may ask, what has all of this got to do with favour and faith? The answer is clear: firstly, the widow, having accepted the request of the Prophet Elijah and shown her willingness to give to him first, demonstrated her faith in God through the prophet. Thus she and her family had enough to eat throughout the famine. On other hand, Naaman, even though he was a Syrian and a pagan, listened to the servant girl when she spoke to him about the Prophet Elisha in Israel whom she said was able to heal him. Naaman welcomed the new Age of the Prophets and straightaway made his way to Israel, which resulted in him being healed.

In short, Jesus referred to these two stories because in the days of Elijah, Israel, led by King Ahab, had turned its back on God and was carrying out evil deeds. This is why Elijah prayed that there should be no rain until he prayed again. This brought about a great famine, during which the land produced nothing. Only one woman, a widow, as she was preparing the last meal for herself and her son before surrendering to death, demonstrated her faith in the prophet and her belief in the words of the prophet. While many others may have ignored the warnings, this woman, through her belief in God, risked believing in the prophet, which paid off.

1 Kings 17:14–15 tells us this, "For this is what the LORD, the God of Israel, says: 'The jar of flour will not be used up and the jug of oil will not run dry

until the day the LORD sends rain on the land.' She went away and did as Elijah had told her. So there was food every day for Elijah and for the woman and her family." Don't you think, as I do, that even though the prophet told her "The jar of flour will not be used up and the jug of oil will not run dry until the day the LORD sends rain on the land", it was her faith in the words of the Prophet Elijah that made her do as he asked and leave.

As to the Syrian Naaman, on other hand, we are told in 2 Kings 5:1–3 "Now Naaman, commander of the army of the King of Syria, was a great and honourable man in the eyes of his master, because by him the LORD had given victory to Syria. He was also a mighty man of valour, *but* a leper. And the Syrians had gone out on raids, and had brought back captive a young girl from the land of Israel. She waited on Naaman's wife. Then she said to her mistress, 'If only my master *were* with the prophet who *is* in Samaria! For he would heal him of his leprosy.'"

Reading further, one then understands just how quickly Naaman responded to the young girl's news, for he went immediately to Israel. Verse 14 records his response to the instruction given to him by the prophet: "So he went down and dipped seven times in the Jordan, according to the saying of the man of God; and his flesh was restored like the flesh of a little child, and he was clean". This story also cements Jesus' claim that there were many people with leprosy in Israel. This is because they did not believe they could be healed and did not believe in the prophet either; none of them went to the prophet for healing as the Syrian had. That is why Naaman alone, because of his faith in the prophet, was healed.

What Jesus was telling his audience in the synagogue is this: in the same way that many people – but not the widow of Zarephath and Naaman the Syrian – were denied God's favour in the days of Elijah and Elisha, so you too will be denied favour that leads to salvation, since you have rejected Me, Jesus, God's ultimate favour. Rejecting Jesus means rejecting God's favour.

THE DANGERS OR THE RISKS OF FAVOUR

It is said that wherever there is sugar there are also ants; it is also said that wherever there are flowers there are also butterflies. My study of favour has shown me that wherever there is favour there is also jealousy, hatred and opposition. In this part of the book, I would like to draw your attention to some examples of jealousy, hatred, and opposition that have been accorded to those who have experienced the favour of God. I do this so that you will not be surprised or panicked when you face any of these incidents in your life as a favoured child of God. Also note that not everybody will be happy because of your progress, some people will be provoked by your growth, happiness, and success.

I think I am right to point out that the danger or risks resulting from favour are natural; that is, favour always comes with associated dangers or risks, either from inside the person or from outside influences. From almost all the stories we have considered earlier in this book about those who were favoured, it is clear that almost all of these people experienced jealousy, hatred, or opposition from others, or some other kind of trouble in their lives. Some even had their lives threatened. Therefore, so that you are aware, I want you to understand that the favour of God does not take away challenges but attracts them, so that at some point in your life you may well not think that the favour of God has left you. You may not realise that the very reason why you are struggling and suffering in life so much is because of the favour of God in your life.

The dangers of favour present themselves in two ways: from outside the person and from within the person. Even though favour is for a lifetime, if care is not taken and a person does not stay within the circle of God's favour, the devil or enemies, by all sorts of means and through any kind of danger, can destroy the person even though s/he is favoured. This is because the devil seeks to destroy twenty-four seven; as Jesus said: "The thief does not come except to steal, and to kill, and to destroy. I have come that they may have life, and that they may have *it* more abundantly" (John

10:10). Therefore it is very important for the child of God to be aware of the devil, know that he works 24/7, and realise the importance of staying within the boundaries of God's favour. Always be aware that favour may attract trouble, but the good news is that favour cannot be defeated, so long as those who are favoured stay within the boundaries of God's favour.

✦ Dangers that come from outside

Jealousy, hatred, back-biting, and opposition are just some of the outside dangers of favour. Take jealousy: jealousy or envy makes people bitter and unhappy about what others have. It makes them feel a certain hatred and bitterness towards anyone who is shown favour or kindness. This is not because of anything the person who has gained favour has done, but only because the advantages, possessions, or position given to the favoured makes others wish they had been given these too.

✦ Abel

Abel was hated by his older brother, Cain, who later murdered him. Cain did not murder his brother because Abel had done anything wrong or had acted against him; he did it because God had looked on Abel's sacrifice with favour (Genesis 4:4–5).

After the LORD had favoured Abraham and called him from among his pagan people (Genesis 12:1–3), the LORD then promised to bless Abraham and make him a great nation (Genesis 15:13). Then the LORD tells Abraham (Abraham is called Abram at this time) the price his descendants will have to pay for the favour: "Then the LORD said to him, 'Know for certain that for four hundred years your descendants will be strangers in a country not their own and that they will be enslaved and mistreated there.'"

The descendants of Abraham (who later are called Israel or the Israelites), for the sake of Jacob, will be slaves, and experience mistreatment in another country for four hundred years.

✦ Joseph

Joseph's father loved him more than all of his brothers, because Joseph was favoured by God. Genesis 37:3 says: "Now Israel loved Joseph more than any of his other sons, because he had been born to him in his old age; and he made a richly ornamented robe for him."

Genesis 37:4 makes clear that hardship, danger, or risk are attached to God's favour for Joseph: "when his brothers saw that their father loved him more than any of them, they hated him and could not be at peace with him." Joseph's brothers try to kill him, they put him in a pit to try to bury his dreams, they speak falsely of him, and later they sold him into slavery. But from slavery to prison, wherever Joseph goes, the favour of God is with him. Joseph found favour with men, until finally he is released from prison to become the Prime Minister of Egypt, through God's divine plan.

✦ The Israelites

In Exodus 5:4–9 we read what happened after the Israelites had received the message from Moses that the LORD was about to take them out of the slavery to their own land, a land flowing with milk and honey, and where they would govern themselves as a nation. On hearing the news, Pharaoh the King of Egypt, intensified their burden, but this could not stop God from carrying out His plan for them. This is proof enough that hardship doesn't mean you have lost God's favour.

"But the King of Egypt said, 'Moses and Aaron, why are you taking the people away from their labour? Get back to your work!' Then Pharaoh said, 'Look, the people of the land are now numerous, and you are stopping them from working.' That same day Pharaoh gave this order to the slave drivers and foremen in charge of the people: 'You are no longer to supply the people with straw for making bricks; let them go and gather their own straw. But require them to make the same number of bricks as before; don't reduce the quota. They are lazy; that is why they are crying out, "Let us go and sacrifice to our God." Make the work harder for the men so that they keep working and pay no attention to lies.'" (Exodus 5:4–9)

The challenges that are thrown up as a result of God's favour can be frustrating and disturbing at times; just when you think you are on your way out of your problem you realise, in fact, that you have been plunged into even more serious trouble. At times such as these, it is easy to think that the LORD has abandoned you, but He has not. Remember that during exams or tests teachers are always silent, but their silent does not mean they lack concern, rather that they are keeping watch. So when God seems silent during your test because of your favour, it does not mean He has abandoned you. Remember that He is keeping watch over you; He is supervising your test. Remember His words of comfort in Psalms 91:15: "He shall call upon Me, and I will answer him; I *will be* with him in trouble; I will deliver him and honour him. Don't panic, for you are in safe hands says the LORD!"

My personal testimony as a Pastor as to the outside dangers, which I believe many ministers, especially those in smaller size churches or ministries experience, is that sometimes, when you look at your congregation during services and see how the Spirit of God is moving among you, one becomes very happy, but during other services, if you are not too careful, you will question your call. In addition, sometimes, the very people you truly believe will not fail you no matter what, or when everybody else has failed you, will be the very people to desert you in the middle of the sea. But let me assure every man or woman of God who may be reading this book that if you are really called by God you need not worry, for He who has called you will also make provision for the perfection of his work. As Paul said, "He who has begun good work in you will surely accomplish what he began."

✦ Jacob

Jacob was favoured and chosen by God when he and his big brother were still in their mother's womb (Genesis 25:22–23; Romans 9:13), and yet even he experienced much suffering in his life.

First, Jacob ran for his life, from among his family at home, to go and live with his uncle, Laban. This was as his mother, Rebekah, suggested because he had grabbed the birthright and the blessing from his elder brother Esau (Genesis 27:41–46). Verse 41 says: "So Esau hated Jacob because of the blessing with which his father blessed him, and Esau said in his heart, 'The days of mourning for my father are at hand; then I will kill my brother Jacob.'"

Secondly, Jacob suffered greatly at the hands of his uncle, Laban and, in Genesis 31:38–42, he confronts his uncle with the ordeal he experienced at his hands; an ordeal that lasted for twenty years. This is what he says to Laban, his uncle: "I have been with you for twenty years now. Your sheep and goats have not miscarried, nor have I eaten rams from your flocks. I did not bring you animals torn by wild beasts; I bore the loss myself. And you demanded payment from me for whatever was stolen by day or night. This was my situation: The heat consumed me in the daytime and the cold at night, and sleep fled from my eyes. It was like this for the twenty years I was in your household. I worked for fourteen years for your two daughters and six years for your flocks, and you changed my wages ten times. If the God of my father, the God of Abraham and the Fear of Isaac, had not been with me, you would surely have sent me away empty-handed.

But God has seen my hardship and the toil of my hands, and last night he rebuked you."

What a joy to know that no matter how terrible Laban's ill-treatment, still Jacob prospered and left fully blessed with cattle and people. This is because God's favour was upon his life. If you have been treated unfairly by anybody, if you are denied anything because of someone's wickedness, if anybody has taken advantage of you because you are at his or her mercy, take consolation from Jacob's story that no one can curse what the LORD has blessed you with. Thus, as a favoured child of God, cheer up, for your deliverance is certain, no matter what your enemies have planned against you.

Never forgetting his encounter with God, Jacob held on to the angel of the LORD and would not let him go until he had blessed him, which is what led to Jacob's name-change to Israel.

This was the result of Jacob's trust in the LORD: the LORD had asked Jacob to return home after many years, but Jacob was frightened, knowing that he would have to face his big brother, who had wanted to kill him when they were young because Jacob had stolen his brother Esau's birthright and blessing. However, Jacob remained faithful in the LORD and faced up to his fears, which earned him even more favour from God (Genesis 32:22–32).

✦ David

As we learned earlier, under the heading "The favour of God will take you to the palace", David was favourably chosen by God and anointed as king. David was chosen from among everyone eligible to take the throne after King Saul, even though he was the youngest of eight sons, who had been rejected by his father, and been made to work as a shepherd (1 Samuel 16).

David's favour attracted very many difficult times for him, such as when he suffered at the hands of King Saul, who repeatedly tried to kill David after he was favoured and had been chosen and anointed to be Saul's successor as King of Israel. But no matter how many times, or what form his enemy's actions took, David survived and was crowned king just as the LORD had promised him.

It is fascinating and wonderful to read in 1 Samuel 16:13–14 that the Spirit of the LORD had departed from Saul and that the Spirit of God was now powerfully on David: "So Samuel took the horn of oil and anointed him in the presence of his brothers, and from that day on the Spirit of the LORD came powerfully upon David. Samuel then went to Ramah. Now the Spirit of the LORD had departed from Saul, and an evil spirit from the LORD tormented him."

For me, the interest lies in David's service to Saul when the evil spirit from the LORD torments him. In verse 23 we read that, "Whenever the spirit from God came on Saul, David would take up his lyre and play. Then relief would come to Saul; he would feel better, and the evil spirit would leave him."

In 1 Samuel 17 we read of David as a young boy: how he killed the Philistine giant Goliath of Gath, and how this brought a great victory to the Israelites against their enemies, the Philistines, in the battle at Ella Valley. Once again I am glad to tell you that twice have I stood in Ella Valley while on a tour of the Holy Land. I pray that one day you, as a believer, will also have the opportunity to visit this wonderful place in Israel at least once in your lifetime.

We also learn how, without consideration for any of the service young David had rendered to him, Saul becomes jealous of David. Saul harbours a very bitter hatred towards David. Between 1 Samuel 17 and 30, we read of the many attempts by Saul to kill David.

David ends up having to run for his life: first he fled to Michal and then to Samuel at Ramah (1 Samuel 19:13–18). From verses 20–24, it is interesting to note how Saul, who is still looking to kill David, ends up prophesying in Naioth at Ramah after his messengers had earlier become prophets too.

1 Samuel 19:23–24 reads: "So Saul went to Naioth at Ramah. But the Spirit of God came even on him, and he walked along prophesying until he came to Naioth. He stripped off his garments, and he too prophesied in Samuel's presence. He lay naked all that day and all that night. This is why people say, 'Is Saul also among the prophets?'"

In 1 Samuel 20 we read that, because Jonathan, Saul's son, had made friends with David he tries to persuade his father to change his mind and stop pursuing his wish to murder David. When David hears of this, he runs even further.

Nothing more is heard of David until 1 Samuel 21:1–9, where we meet him again at Nob and then at Gath, the city from which Goliath came. Here, having been refused by the King of the Philistines (maybe because the king had some concerns about David the giant-slayer), David journeys to a cave in Adullam, where it is said 400 men gathered around him and made him their king (22:1–4; 1 Chronicles 12:8–18).

"David left Gath and escaped to the cave of Adullam. When his brothers and his father's household heard about it, they went down to him there. All those who were in distress or in debt or discontented gathered around him, and he became their commander. About four hundred men were with him." (1 Samuel 22:1–2)

We also learn that, at this time, David longed for and cried out for water from his home town of Bethlehem, but when three of his own men risked their lives to fetch him water from there he would not drink it (Samuel 23:13–17).

We also learn that this happened during the period when, in his failure to capture and murder David, Saul ordered Doeg the Edomite to kill eighty-five priests in Nob. The news was delivered to David by Abiathar, a son of Ahimelech.

1 Samuel 22:16-20

"But the king said, 'You will surely die, Ahimelech, you and your whole family.' Then the king ordered the guards at his side: 'Turn and kill the priests of the LORD, because they too have sided with David. They knew he was fleeing, yet they did not tell me.' But the king's officials were unwilling to raise a hand to strike the priests of the LORD. The king then ordered Doeg, 'You turn and strike down the priests.' So Doeg the Edomite turned and struck them down. That day he killed eighty-five men who wore the linen ephod. He also put to the sword Nob, the town of the priests, with its men and women, its children and infants, and its cattle, donkeys and sheep. But one son of Ahimelech son of Ahitub, named Abiathar, escaped and fled to join David."

It is said that as a result of this news, David composed Psalm 52.

Jonathan visits and encourages David (23:16–18), but the sad news is that this was the last meeting between the two men, as Jonathan later dies in battle with his father and his two brothers.

✦ Chapter 24: David spares Saul's life

For me, this is a really intriguing part of David and Saul's story, when David refuses to kill Saul, because he is the LORD's anointed, even though the LORD has delivered him into his hands. "After Saul returned from pursuing the Philistines, he was told, 'David is in the Desert of En Gedi.' So Saul took three thousand able young men from all Israel and set out to look for David and his men near the Crags of the Wild Goats. He came to the sheep pens along the way; a cave was there, and Saul went in to relieve himself. David and his men were far back in the cave. The men said, 'This is the day the LORD spoke of when he said to you, "I will give your enemy into your hands for you to deal with as you wish."' **Then David crept up unnoticed and cut off a corner of Saul's robe.** Afterward, David was conscience-stricken for having cut off a corner of his robe. He said to his men, 'The LORD forbid that I should do such a thing to my master, the LORD's anointed, or lay my hand on him; for he is the anointed of the LORD.' With these words David sharply rebuked his men and did not allow them to attack Saul. And Saul left the cave and went his way. Then David went out of the cave and called out to Saul, 'My lord the king!' When Saul looked behind him, David bowed down and prostrated himself with his face to the ground." (1 Samuel 24:1–8)

✦ Chapter 25

This chapter records David's encounter with Nabal and Abigail.

✦ Chapter 26

David again spares Saul's life because the LORD had put him and his men into a deep sleep. Again he insisted that "the LORD forbid that I should lay a hand on the LORD's anointed."

In 1 Samuel 26:6–12 we read:

"David then asked Ahimelech the Hittite and Abishai son of Zeruiah, Joab's brother, 'Who will go down into the camp with me to Saul?' 'I'll go with you,' said Abishai. So David and Abishai went to the army by night, and there was Saul, lying asleep inside the camp with his spear stuck in the ground near his head. Abner and the soldiers were lying around him. Abishai said to David, 'Today God has delivered your enemy into your hands. Now let me pin him to the ground with one thrust of the spear; I won't strike him twice.' But David said to Abishai, 'Don't destroy him! Who can lay a hand on the LORD's anointed and be guiltless? As surely as the LORD lives,' he said, 'the LORD himself will strike him, or his time will come and he will die, or he will go into battle and perish. But the LORD forbids that I should lay a hand on the LORD's anointed. Now get the spear and water jug that are near his head, and let's go.' ***So David took the spear and water jug near Saul's head, and they left.*** No one saw or knew about it, nor did anyone wake up. They were all sleeping, because the LORD had put them into a deep sleep."

✦ Chapter 27

David did finally settle among the Philistines and was welcomed by the king who, upon David's request, assigned to him Ziklag as his residence. Verse 4 tells us, "When Saul was told that David had fled to Gath, he no longer searched for him."

1 Samuel 27:1-7

"But David thought to himself, 'One of these days I will be destroyed by the hand of Saul. The best thing I can do is to escape to the land of the Philistines. Then Saul will give up searching for me anywhere in Israel, and I will slip out of his hand.' So David and the six hundred men with him left and went over to Achish son of Maok King of Gath. David and his men settled in Gath with Achish. Each man had his family with him, and David had his two wives: Ahinoam of Jezreel and Abigail of Carmel, the widow of Nabal. When

Saul was told that David had fled to Gath, he no longer searched for him. Then David said to Achish, 'If I have found favour in your eyes, let a place be assigned to me in one of the country towns, that I may live there. Why should your servant live in the royal city with you?' So on that day Achish gave him Ziklag, and it has belonged to the kings of Judah ever since. David lived in Philistine territory a year and four months."

✦ Chapter 28

We are informed that Saul consults a medium at Endor.

Verses 1–7

"In those days the Philistines gathered their forces to fight against Israel. Achish said to David, 'You must understand that you and your men will accompany me in the army.' David said, 'Then you will see for yourself what your servant can do.' Achish replied, 'Very well, I will make you my bodyguard for life.' Now Samuel was dead, and all Israel had mourned for him and buried him in his own town of Ramah. Saul had expelled the mediums and spiritists from the land. The Philistines assembled and came and set up camp at Shunem, while Saul gathered all Israel and set up camp at Gilboa. When Saul saw the Philistine army, he was afraid; terror filled his heart. He inquired of the LORD, but the LORD did not answer him by dreams or Urim or prophets. Saul then said to his attendants, 'Find me a woman who is a medium, so I may go and inquire of her.'"

Reading further from verse 7, we learn how Saul, in disguise, goes to visit a medium woman. The woman sees Samuel and identifies him by name. Saul asks the woman to bring to him the man she sees, but the woman is fearful now that she knows it is Saul she is talking to, because previously, before she'd seen through his disguise, she had told him that the king had killed all the priests and the spiritists. Saul tells the woman not to fear and then he requests that she brings Samuel to him:

"When the woman saw Samuel, she cried out at the top of her voice and said to Saul, 'Why have you deceived me? You are Saul!' The king said to her, 'Don't be afraid. What do you see?' The woman said, 'I see a ghostly figure coming up out of the earth.' 'What does he look like?' he asked. 'An old man wearing a robe is coming up,' she said. Then Saul knew it was Samuel, and he bowed down and prostrated himself with his face to the ground. Samuel said to Saul, 'Why have you disturbed me by bringing me up?' 'I am in great distress,' Saul said. 'The Philistines are fighting against me, and God has departed from me. He no longer answers me, either by prophets or by dreams. So I have called on you to tell me what to do.' Samuel said, 'Why do you consult me, now that the LORD has departed from you and become your enemy? The LORD has done what he predicted through me. The LORD has torn the kingdom out of your hands and given it to one of your neighbours—to David. Because you did not obey the LORD or carry out his fierce wrath against the Amalekites, the LORD has done this to you today. The LORD will deliver both Israel and you into the hands of the Philistines, and tomorrow you and your sons will be with me. The LORD will also give the army of Israel into the hands of the Philistines.'" (1 Samuel 28:12–19)

✦ Chapter 29

This is another interesting story, where we learn that after David had lived at Ziklag for a year with his men the king, Achish, asked them to join his army in a war against Saul, which they did.

In verses 2–5 we read: "As the Philistine rulers marched with their units of hundreds and thousands, David and his men were marching at the rear with Achish. The commanders of the Philistines asked, 'What about these Hebrews?' Achish replied, 'Is this not David, who was an officer of Saul King of Israel? He has already been with me for over a year, and from the day he left Saul until now, I have found no fault in him.' But the Philistine commanders were angry with Achish and said, 'Send the man back that he may return to the place you assigned him. He must not go with us into battle, or he will turn against us during the fighting. How better could he regain his master's favour than by taking the heads of our own men? Isn't this the David they sang about in their dances: "Saul has slain his thousands, and David his tens of thousands"?' With this the king listened to the advice of his commanders so he sent David and his men back to Ziklag.

✦ Chapter 30

This chapter continues the story, with David Destroying the Amalekites.

David's troubles multiply as we are told in verses 1–6: "David and his men reached Ziklag on the third day. Now the Amalekites had raided the Negev and Ziklag. They had attacked Ziklag and burned it, and had taken captive the women and everyone else in it, both young and old. They killed none of them, but carried them off as they went on their way. When David and his men reached Ziklag, they found it destroyed by fire and their wives and sons and daughters taken captive. So David and his men wept aloud until they had no strength left to weep. David's two wives had been captured—Ahinoam of Jezreel and Abigail, the widow of Nabal of Carmel. David was greatly distressed because the men were talking of stoning him; each one was bitter in spirit because of his sons and daughters. But David found strength in the Lord his God."

✦ Chapter 31

This chapter records the death of Saul and his sons, just as Samuel had predicted when Saul consulted the medium, as we read earlier in 28:17–19:

"The Lord has done what he predicted through me. The Lord has torn the kingdom out of your hands and given it to one of your neighbours—to David. Because you did not obey the Lord or carry out his fierce wrath against the Amalekites, the Lord has done this to you today. The Lord will deliver both Israel and you into the hands of the Philistines, and tomorrow you and your sons will be with me. The Lord will also give the army of Israel into the hands of the Philistines."

✦ 2 Samuel, Chapter 2

After the death of Saul, David was anointed King over Judah, the southern kingdom.

In 2 Samuel 2:1–4 we read how, "In the course of time, David inquired of the LORD. 'Shall I go up to one of the towns of Judah?' he asked. The LORD said, 'Go up.' David asked, 'Where shall I go?' 'To Hebron,' the LORD answered. So David went up there with his two wives, Ahinoam of Jezreel and Abigail, the widow of Nabal of Carmel. David also took the men who were with him, each with his family, and they settled in Hebron and its towns. Then the men of Judah came to Hebron, and there they anointed David king over the tribe of Judah."

✦ 2 Samuel, Chapter 5

David is crowned King of Israel, the northern kingdom.

2 Samuel 5:1–3 and 1 Samuel 11:1–3

In 2 Samuel 5:1–3 we read: "All the tribes of Israel came to David at Hebron and said, 'We are your own flesh and blood. In the past, while Saul was king over us, you were the one who led Israel on their military campaigns. And the LORD said to you, "You will shepherd my people Israel, and you will become their ruler.'" When all the elders of Israel had come to King David at Hebron, the king made a covenant with them at Hebron before the LORD, and they anointed David King over Israel."

What is the essence of this narrative about David's troubles at the hands of Saul? I believe that it is to let us know that as we seek the LORD's favour we will become aware that there are dangers associated with doing so as well.

According to the theologians, David was seventeen years old when he was anointed by Samuel and he was thirty years old when he ascended to the throne. This means that it took thirteen years of running from Saul before David was crowned King of Israel.

✦ Esther and the Jews at Susa

We also learn of Esther: after she had won the favour of God and been honoured in a foreign land to become queen, her life, and that of all her people, the Jews, was threatened by Haman, because he wanted all the Jews killed. But yet again, Esther's life and the lives of all the Jews were preserved by God when Haman's evil plot backfired on him.

✦ Nehemiah

My interest lies now in the details of the dangers that face Nehemiah after he received favour from the king to go back to Jerusalem to build the broken walls of the city.

Nehemiah won the favour of the king, who not only gave him permission to go back to Jerusalem to build the walls and the gates of the city, but also gave him all the necessary support to carry out his task, but Nehemiah also faced great opposition.

We read in Nehemiah 2:9–10 that Nehemiah said: "So I went to the governors of Trans-Euphrates and gave them the king's letters. The king had also sent army officers and cavalry with me. When Sanballat the Horonite and Tobiah the Ammonite official heard about this, they were very much disturbed that someone had come to promote the welfare of the Israelites". You see, not all people will be happy of your favour or your success.

Nehemiah's response is retold in verses 19–20: "But when Sanballat the Horonite, Tobiah the Ammonite official, and Geshem the Arab heard about it, they mocked and ridiculed us. 'What is this you are doing?'

they asked. 'Are you rebelling against the king?' I answered them by saying, 'The God of heaven will give us success. We his servants will start rebuilding, but as for you, you have no share in Jerusalem or any claim or historic right to it.'"

Nehemiah's response to the opposition shows how confident he was that the God who had given him favour would also ensure him success. How confident are you in the LORD your God? Can you, in the face of opposition such as that which Nehemiah faced, declare:"I know my God will ensure my success?"The way in which you handle any type of danger you face in life, because of the favour of God, will determine either your success or defeat.

Nehemiah 4: 1–3, tells how Sanballat and Tobias now turned their opposition into mockery in an attempt to discourage and distract the builders: "When Sanballat heard that we were rebuilding the wall, he became angry and was greatly incensed. He ridiculed the Jews, and in the presence of his associates and the army of Samaria, he said, 'What are those feeble Jews doing? Will they restore their wall? Will they offer sacrifices? Will they finish in a day? Can they bring the stones back to life from those heaps of rubble—burned as they are?' Tobiah the Ammonite, who was at his side, said, 'What they are building—even a fox climbing up on it would break down their wall of stones!'"

But again, Nehemiah responds to their mockery by committing the situation into the hands of God, as we learn in Nehemiah 4: 4–5: "Nehemiah prayed saying: 'Hear us, our God, for we are despised. Turn their insults back on their own heads. Give them over as plunder in a land of captivity. Do not cover up their guilt or blot out their sins from your sight, for they have thrown insults in the face of the builders.'"

How do you respond when you are ridiculed by your enemies? We all face ridicule of many kinds in our life, but the only way to cope with ridicule is through faith.

In Nehemiah 4: 7–9 we see how the opposition intensifies when Nehemiah and his men refuse to give up, but once again Nehemiah reacts with prayer: "But when Sanballat, Tobiah, the Arabs, the Ammonites and the people of Ashdod heard that the repairs to Jerusalem's walls had gone ahead and that the gaps were being closed, they were very angry. They all plotted together to come and fight against Jerusalem and stir up trouble against it. But we prayed to our God and posted a guard day and night to meet this threat."

Sometimes, as a favoured child of God, the opposition will intensify even when you are expecting it to subside because you have prayed. Take a lesson from Nehemiah, keep on praying, and never give up! Your God will give you victory if you hold on to Him.

In Nehemiah 4:15–23 we read - quite against what many of us would have done in response to the intensity of the opposition - that Nehemiah and his men intensify their efforts, working day and night. Learn from this, and reflect on the many times when, instead of intensifying our efforts and concentrating on what we are doing, we turn to the enemies' distractions. Realise that this is simply a waste of time and that it is designed to divert your attention from what the LORD has called you to do.

In Nehemiah 6:15–17 we see how the enemies' evil plans develop in order to get Nehemiah and his men to stop work. But no matter their efforts to persuade him, Nehemiah could not be persuaded: Nehemiah even refuses their offer of a peace meeting and did not fall for their trick to get at him through a false prophecy, because he suspected that it was all just an evil plot to capture and kill him. In spite of all the opposition, Nehemiah and his men completed the work that he had received favour to carry out, just as

Daniel had predicted in Daniel 9:25: "The wall was completed in 52 days."

To conclude the discussion of Nehemiah's story, let me say to you that in life, as favoured children of God, we will face actions like those of Sanballat and Tobiah. Every day, even in our churches, there are people with the spirit of Sanballat and Tobiah, always opposing the peoples' interest and always ready to oppose the interests of the church. Thank God, however, that He always ensures us victory over such enemies at all times (1 Corinthians 15:57).

✦ Daniel and his three Hebrew friends

Daniel and his three Hebrew friends, having been honoured in a foreign land as a result of God's favour, also faced the danger of favour. Daniel was dumped into the lions' den and his friends were thrown into a blazing furnace, but still they all came out unharmed (Daniel 6:16–23 and 3:22–27 respectively).

✦ Mary, Jesus' mother

In Luke 1:26–32, as we studied earlier, Mary received the highest favour from God because she was chosen to be the mother of Jesus Christ, God's ultimate favour for mankind, but, as a result, she also faced the troubles that come with favour. In Luke 2:34–35 we read: "Then Simeon blessed them and said to Mary, his mother: 'This child is destined to cause the falling and rising of many in Israel, and to be a sign that will be spoken against, so that the thoughts of many hearts will be revealed. And a sword will pierce your own soul too.'"

This prophecy of Simeon is read in two forms: (1) it tells of the impact Jesus was going to make on the Jews; because of Him some would fall and others would rise, and (2), it relates implicitly to this part of the book, because Simeon said to Mary the mother of Jesus that the sword would pierce her own soul, by which he meant that the sorrow she would feel or which would come upon her was as a result of the suffering that Jesus would experience. Remember, that as Jesus' mother, the pain and horror Mary went through when Jesus was betrayed and arrested was unbearable; and then when Barabbas was released and Jesus was condemned to death, when he was flogged and finally crucified, her pain must have been immense and I am beginning to think that, even though it is not recorded, Mary may have remembered what Simeon had told her. But remember as well that, even though very little is recorded, Mary's joy on that faithful Sunday when Jesus rose from the dead must have been even greater than the pain and sorrow she had felt previously.

✦ Jesus Christ

Did you know that on the day Jesus Christ declared the year of the Lord's favour in Luke chapter 4, the Jews wanted to kill him on that very day? Verses 28–30 say: "All the people in the synagogue were furious when they heard this. They got up, drove him out of the town, and took him to the brow of the hill on which the town was built, in order to throw him off the cliff. But he walked right through the crowd and went on his way." (Luke 4:28–30, NIV)

As I said earlier, when you are favoured, even though it is not your fault, you will attract hatred, hardship and troubles, which sometimes could even threaten your life. Others will be jealous of you, you may be envied by others. The people of Galilee wanted to kill Jesus because he claimed to be the fulfilment of Isaiah's prophecy, but he walked away, because his time of death was not due. Never mind, therefore, when people hate or envy you, as these are signs that you are favoured. Even if your life is threatened, no one can kill you before your time. If Jesus walked away unharmed, you too will walk away unharmed from any plans your enemies have to plot against you, in Jesus' name.

✦ Dangers from within

The possibility of falling from favour is one of several dangers that present themselves as a result of God's favour. Tenet No. 10 of The Apostolic Church warns against the possibility of falling from grace. What this means is that it is possible that a believer can lose or fall from His salvation if due care is not taken. As part of this section on the dangers of favour, I would like to say to you that there is a possibility of falling from favour unless you take due care; it is possible for one to abuse favour and therefore fall from favour. Favour is like salvation, yet even though favour lasts for a lifetime, personally I believe that as believers, the favoured must stay in Christ and His word, in order to maintain His favour.

Unlike, as discussed previously, when the dangers come from outside or external sources, here, we are discussing danger that comes from within. The source of the danger is internal, coming from within the man himself. I want to say to you that the dangers of favour which are inside a person are far more dangerous than those that come from outside. Some of these inside dangers come from a lack of self-control, which can lead to things like pride and lust.

✦ King David abused his favour

Remember, as already discussed under the heading "The favour of God will take you to the palace", David was favourably chosen and anointed as king to take the throne after King Saul, this is even though he was the youngest son among his father's eight sons, was rejected by his father, and sent out to work as a shepherd (1 Samuel 16).

In this part of the book, we will treat this same man, David, who after surviving a series of difficult times then suffered at the hands of King Saul. Saul repeatedly tried to kill David because of the favour of God upon his life. Sadly, after been crowned king, David abused the favour granted to him when he neglected his duties and left himself open to criticism.

In 2 Samuel 11:1–3 we are informed that "It happened in the spring of the year, at the time when kings go out *to battle*, that David sent Joab and his servants with him, and all Israel; and they destroyed the people of Ammon and besieged Rabbah. But David remained at Jerusalem. Then it happened one evening that David arose from his bed and walked on the roof of the king's house. And from the roof he saw a woman bathing, and the woman *was* very beautiful to behold. So David sent and inquired about the woman. And *someone* said, 'Is this not Bathsheba, the daughter of Eliam, the wife of Uriah the Hittite?'"

The quotation above is our key text for this part of the book. The message it is providing is one about responsibility: King David was supposed to be at war with the kings; in fact, he was supposed to command his army as Commander in Chief, but he neglected his duties and stayed at home in Jerusalem instead, while the entire Israelite army went to fight the Ammonites without their leader.

The Bible, good as it is, does not make any attempt at hiding sin or any of the mistakes made by the main characters, not in the slightest, for it records everything, either good or bad, about all the main characters.

Further reading of the scripture reveals that it is during this time that David's lust of the eye leads him to commit one of the greatest sins recorded in the Bible.

Verses 2 & 3 and further

To summarise what happens next, which may be a warning to us all, we are shown that there are lasting consequences to David's fall. Bathsheba became pregnant from their adulterous liaison. Fearing discovery of his sin and shame David sent for Uriah, the husband of Bathsheba, with the hope that Uriah would go home and sleep with Bathsheba. But Uriah, in contrast to David, showed integrity: "Uriah said to David, 'The ark and Israel and Judah are staying in tents, and my master Joab and my lord's men are camped in the open fields. How could I go to my house to eat and drink and lie with my wife? As surely as you live, I will not do such a thing!'" (2 Samuel 11:11)

David's next scheme was to convince Uriah to stay for a day so that he could try and get Uriah drunk. Uriah still didn't go home, but "slept on a mat among his master's servants" (2 Samuel 11:14). Growing impatient with the situation David writes a letter to Joab, which he gives to Uriah to deliver, which Uriah does faithfully, unaware that the letter sealed his own doom and that it represented his death warrant. David wrote: "Put Uriah in the front line where the fighting is fiercest. Then withdraw from him so he will be struck down and die." (2 Samuel 11:14)

Consequently Uriah is killed by the Ammonites, and after the standard period of mourning, David married Bathsheba. However, as the Bible warns: "But the thing David had done displeased the Lord." (2 Samuel 11:25)

Because of the Lord's displeasure, we see the lasting, generational consequences. The Prophet Nathan came to David and told him what the Lord had said about the consequences of what he had done: "Why did you despise the word of the Lord by doing what is evil in his eyes? You struck down Uriah the Hittite with the sword and took his wife to be your own. You killed him with the sword of the Ammonites. Now, therefore, the sword will never depart from your house, because you despised me and took the wife of Uriah the Hittite to be your own. This is what the Lord says: 'Out of your own household I am going to bring calamity upon you. Before your very eyes I will take your wives and give them to one who is close to you, and he will lie with your wives in broad daylight. You did it in secret, but I will do this thing in broad daylight before all Israel.' Then David said to Nathan, 'I have sinned against the Lord.' Nathan replied, 'The Lord has taken away your sin. You are not going to die. But because by doing this you have made the enemies of the Lord show utter contempt, the son born to you will die.'" (2 Samuel 2:9–14)

The effect of David's abuse of his favour accorded him enormous suffering, despite his earnest repentance. This prompts David to write Psalm 51, where he laments that everything the LORD spoke of happened. The foundation David laid down by his actions affected generations after him very badly: the child born to David and Bathsheba died (2 Samuel 12:15–18); Amnon, David's first-born son, raped his own half-sister, Tamar (2 Samuel 13:28–29); Amnon is killed by his half-brother, Absalom (2 Samuel 13:28–29); Absalom rebels against his father, David, and sleeps with ten of his father's concubines (2 Samuel 16:20–23); Absalom was killed by Joab when his long flowing hair, or more probably his head, was caught in the bough of an oak tree during his rebellion against his father (2:14); and Adonijah, David's fourth son, was executed on the orders of his half-brother Solomon (1 Kings 2:13–25).

Some of these terrible occurrences can happen to any of us if we abuse the favour of God in our life. We are all vulnerable to what we see, but the lesson I am trying to teach you here is that, although you may not be able to stop your eyes from looking, you can resist further wrongful behaviour, such as we witness by David's action after he saw Bathsheba's nakedness. To be tempted is not sinful, but your wrongful actions after, like David's with Bathsheba, is sinful. Nevertheless, if you are reading this book and find yourself in the devil's trap because you did not exercise self-control, God is willing to forgive you any iniquity you have committed, just as he did David, but only if, like David, you willingly and honestly admit your mistake and are ready to repent.

✦ Solomon abused his favour

King Solomon was favoured by God and was chosen to succeed his father as the King of Israel, regardless of the background that led to his parents' marriage, and like his father, he was also the youngest among his father's sons.

Solomon was a great and good king who received his religious training from the Prophet Nathan, who gave him the name *Jedidiah*, meaning "the LORD's daring" (2 Samuel 12:25). His kingdom began in a blaze of glory. 1 Kings 4 records that his cabinet was greater than any king Israel had ever had. Solomon was the man who asked for, and then received wisdom, along with other things, from God.

The climax of Solomon's kingship is his lifework of building the Temple for the LORD, an achievement his father, David, desired to do for the LORD, but which the LORD had refused, saying you are not the one to build me the temple, but your son will build the temple for me.

Unfortunately, the life of this great, wise man of his time, like Saul, the first King of Israel, ended in anti-climax, because his heart was lifted up in pride, one of the characteristics of the inner dangers of favour (1 Kings 10:18–29).

It is sad to note that Solomon, despite the LORD's warning in 1 Kings 11, married many wives and had many concubines, including pagans who led him into idolatry against the LORD's command, for his people, Israel, and all believers, and which was reiterated by Paul in 2 Corinthians 6:14. He said: "Do not be yoked together with unbelievers. For what do righteousness and wickedness have in common? Or what fellowship can light have with darkness." (2 Corinthians 6:14)

Personally, the part of Solomon's life that grieves my soul most is that the man who once built a magnificent Temple for the LORD, in order to appease his pagan wives and concubines, now turns into the builder of pagan temples. This is because he has fallen from the LORD's favour as a result of sin. No wonder, then, that after Solomon's death kingship ceased to be the medium through which God governed his people Israel.

All the scriptures below were written by Solomon, so understand that he is being judged by his own words.

"When pride comes, then comes disgrace, but with humility comes wisdom." (Proverbs 11:2)

"Pride goes before destruction, a haughty spirit before a fall." (Proverbs 16:18)

"Before a downfall the heart is haughty, but humility comes before honour." (Proverbs 18:12)

"Pride brings a person low, but the lowly in spirit gain honour." (Proverbs 29:23)

As the scriptures record, Solomon was known as the wisest man on earth in his day, yet he failed to live by his own wisdom, what a pity. 1 Kings 4:31–32 records that: "He was wiser than anyone else, including Ethan the Ezrahite—wiser than Heman, Kalkol and Darda, the sons of Mahol. And his fame spread to all the surrounding nations. He spoke three thousand proverbs and his songs numbered a thousand and five."

Many a time when reading or listening to stories like Solomon's, we turn to wonder why and ask questions, such as why Solomon did what he did: what we don't realise is that we all do the same in so many ways. Many people, like Solomon, have fallen from grace to grass because they have fallen from God's favour in their life due to pride.

After King Nebuchadnezzar was humbled by God as a result of his pride, and his sanity had been restored, he had this to say about the one and only true God: "At the same time that my sanity was restored, my honour and splendour were returned to me for the glory of my kingdom. My advisers and nobles sought me out, and I was restored to my throne and became even greater than before. Now I, Nebuchadnezzar, praise and exalt and glorify the King of heaven, because everything he does is right and all his ways are just. And those who walk in pride he is able to humble." (Daniel 4:36–37)

In conclusion of this section, allow me to offer you some good advice: if you have been favoured and honoured, if you have been given any high position or privilege in life, or have prospered in your life, stay loyal to God in order to maintain his favour upon your life. Do not allow your pride to rob you of everything you have. Worse still, do not, like Solomon, begin to do what is evil in the sight of God; if Solomon can err like this then it can happen to anyone, unless due care is taken.

I am aware that there is another danger, when people own but abuse God's favour in their life. Apart from taking advantage of your favour in order to be elevated to a higher position to do evil, another way favour can be abused is when a person refuses to use what God has favourably given to him or her, such as gifts and talents. When this happens, and the person neglects using the favour bestowed on them by God, the individual will be doing something that is not meant for them. This will produce less prosperity and cause them greater struggling.

Allow me to underline this point on favour: when one fails to stay at a location, in a job, or even within a marriage that God has favourably given, remember what the Proverb says: "He who finds a wife finds what is good and receives favour from the Lord." (Proverbs 18:22)

Stay where the Lord, in His favour, has placed you; use the gifts and talents the Lord has given you, and stay with the man or woman the Lord gave you. If you do so, then you will prosper, even in the face of challenges and dangers, for the Lord will always bless what He has given. The favour of God will establish connections in your life; He will bring into your life the people and everything that you need to bring glory to Him.

THOSE WHO RISK THEIR LIFE AND WORK TO FAVOUR OTHERS

As we learnt earlier, favour manifests either when God himself – out of goodwill and bypassing everyone – does something for somebody, even though the person may not deserve it, or have done anything in the past to deserve it. Or God may cause someone to do something for another person out of goodwill; again, even though the person may not deserve it. God, that is, may influence someone to show special kindness, approval, partiality, or honour to a person who many feel may not even qualify. The favour may be a superior showing favour for someone in a low position, but not because the person necessarily deserves it, or even that the person granting the favour wants to do so, but it will be so because God is causing him/her to grant the favour, even should they have to risk their job or even their life to do so.

In this section allow me to share with you some examples from the Bible of people who took a risky decision to grant favour to another person.

Jacob favoured Joseph, and demonstrated his love for him over his other children when he made him a coat of many colours; this was a risk he took for which he paid the price.

Do you realise that when the warder who put Joseph in charge of the prison and made him responsible for all that was done there (Genesis 39:22) did so, that he was risking his life and his job? At the time, if a prisoner in your charge escaped, you were made either to serve their sentence or you paid with your life. But out of God's favour, the warder did not even consider any of these dangers, but put Joseph – someone who had been accused of raping his master's wife – in charge of everything.

There was another warder who risked his life and job by doing something totally against the rules, when he assisted the prisoners he was looking after. This incident is told in Acts 16:29–34, where it says that: "The jailer called for lights, rushed in and fell trembling before Paul and Silas. He then brought them out and asked, 'Sirs, what must I do to be saved?'

They replied, 'Believe in the LORD Jesus, and you will be saved—you and your household.' Then they spoke the word of the LORD to him and to all the others in his house. At that hour of the night the jailer took them and washed their wounds; then immediately he and his household were baptised. The jailer brought them into his house and set a meal before them; he was filled with joy because he had come to believe in God—he and his whole household."

This story, which is foundation scripture for my book *The Power for your Zero Hour,* is all about Paul and Silas who, by the power of the name of Jesus, set free a certain slave girl possessed with a spirit of divination. They were then falsely accused of throwing the city of Athens into an uproar by advocating customs unlawful for Romans to accept or practice, and thus they were arrested, beaten, and imprisoned by the magistrates. However, the Bible says in verses 25–26, "that about mid-night when Paul and Silas prayed and sang praises to the LORD, the LORD answered them with a great earthquake"; this is one of the greatest miracles recorded by the Bible.

Acknowledging this, as we read the earlier verses 29–34, we learn that the jailer or warder brought them out, sent them to his house, and set food before them.

It is then that we realise that the warder was carrying out an extremely risky action, an act of great personal bravery, because under Roman law he could have paid with his life had one of the prisoners escaped. This I see as great personal risk, because a warder was not allowed to favour any prisoner sent to prison by the magistrates. However God, through His miracle, gave Paul and Silas favour before the jailer. This is what favour can do, and will do for you if you believe. When you find favour with someone, when anybody does something for you, they don't consider what will happen next.

CONCLUSION

In conclusion, I would like emphatically to declare that Jesus Christ is God's ultimate favour for mankind. This is why I say that all believers are favoured by God. In Christ dwell all things, when you receive Him you have everything in life, including eternal life. All men were sinners and were therefore separated from God as a result of Adam and Eve's sin of disobedience in the Garden of Eden (Genesis 3), but God sent his only begotten Son Jesus Christ to die on the cross so that all those who believe in Him will be saved (redeemed from the guilt and the power of sin). In Romans 5:8 Paul said: "But God demonstrates his own love for us in this: While we were still sinners, Christ died for us".

While we were not qualified and did not deserve it, still Christ died for us.

Therefore, if you have been reading this book or hearing me preach as an unbeliever, I challenge you: first receive Him into your heart as LORD and Saviour and then all other things will be added unto you. As He said in Matthew 6:33: "But seek first his kingdom and his righteousness, and all these things will be given to you as well". For all the other things Jesus was referring to, return to verse 25 of Matthew, chapter 6.

Favour will attract many things to you, including evil deeds that can lead to sin, but my advice to you is to be like Joseph: know who you are, and flee or run away from all things that are evil. Never yield to anything that attracts you but could result in sin, for sin will separate you from God and take away His favour upon your life. For example, don't yield to the sin of fornication when you are attracted to a man or a woman, saying it is because of your beauty, handsomeness, or because you are rich, forgetting that you are who you are, that you are attractive, only because of God's favour on you.

If you know that you are favoured, and that therefore in life you are attracted to many things or many things are attracted to you, including evil deeds from both outside and inside, then you must always be alert and prayerful, like Nehemiah. For you, like him, may not realise that the reason you are struggling so much in life is because of the favour that is in your life; and you may not understand that this is why the enemy is trying to frustrate you through things like jealousy and hatred from others. After reading this book, from today, I want you to base your life on Psalm 5:12 and other supported quotations. This will help you to know that, as a believer, you are the righteous, whom God has surrounded with favour like a shield, and so you are fully blessed and protected. Constantly meditate on the word of God, for this will enable you to find the right mindset, in order to function as a true favoured child of God.

Because of God's favour, Noah and his family were saved, when the LORD destroyed the earth and everything in it with a Flood. God did this for Noah and his family because Noah was found to be righteous. Because he was favoured, the LORD himself shut the door of the ark behind Noah and his family, so that they were fully secure and protected, and the ark was completely watertight. Did you know that the devil, like water ingress or leakage, can be very difficult to stop or prevent? But when God shuts the door of your life behind you because you are favoured, your life will be both devil-resistant and watertight. It should also be noted that, because of the LORD's favour, not only were Noah and his family saved from the flood, but they were also protected from all the harmful animals that shared the Ark with them.

I want to end this book by giving glory to God once again. I thank Him for His favour upon my life, for calling me from among many as his servant to work in his vineyard as a Minister of the Gospel, even though I did not deserve it, nor can think of anything I have done that is worthy of such an honour. God counted me worthy. As proof to what I am saying, let me tell you about another important event in my journey: when I was called into the ministry I was rejected by the men with whom I was working, because they preferred another person. At that time I was confused and frustrated, and even on the day I was ordained I felt terrible because of the actions of these people. However, to my relief during the service, the Spirit of the LORD spoke words of encouragement to my heart and assured me that as He had called me so He will be with me. And, even though the going has not been easy, yet, He has been with me as He promised and will be with me for evermore. Every word spoken to me has been fulfilled; as I said, things have not been easy, but no matter what and how they come, the LORD has been faithful to me, stage after stage, since The Good

Way Apostolic Church (GWAC) was born. By the grace of God, through The GWAC, we are building a family through the gospel and we are raising an army of believers through God's word. That is, we preach the gospel and we teach the word.

Recently, when I have been preaching in church, almost everybody present has been tearful because of the power of the word and the conviction with which I have ministered through the Holy Spirit. Remember, this is the same person who was rejected by men as not fit for the God's call. I am sharing this with you as a testimony to the fact that because of the favour of God upon your life there will always be opposition, jealousy, and hatred. Never allow any of these things to stop you from being what the LORD has called you to be, for He will always provide you with the lamb for the sacrifice to fulfil whatever He has called you to be.

Always remember also, that as a child of God, the righteous, you are favoured no matter what happens, no matter what others say or think. May the LORD help you to have the mentality of holding His favour in your life and always think, talk, and act as God's favoured child. May the favour of God be upon you in Jesus' name.

Other Publications by Pastor David Amoah

These wonderful books by Pastor David Amoah will help you to preach and to preach effectively, it will help you to reach your potential in the LORD. Through his teachings Pastor David offers his comfort, wisdom and knowledge; with these books the Pastor had brought many into the fold all around the globe.

Temptation

Be Ye Transformed

Stay Connected To Christ

Your Future Is In Your Hands

The Power For Your Zero Hour

Guidelines for Preachers and Teachers of God's Word

CONTACT DETAILS

For more copies of this book and other publications by Pastor David Amoah; to make an appointment for preaching or teaching; for prayer, support and counselling, please contact:

The Good Way Apostolic Church office
110-118 Markfield Road
London N15 4QF
T: 020 8801 4298, **Mob:** 07575230988
E: amoahdla@yahoo.co.uk
W: www.davidamoah.co.uk

www.ingramcontent.com/pod-product-compliance
Lightning Source LLC
Chambersburg PA
CBHW071431080526
44587CB00014B/1803